THE POLITICS OF REALITY: ESSAYS IN FEMINIST THEORY

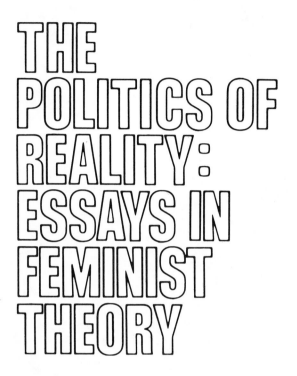

THE POLITICS OF REALITY: ESSAYS IN FEMINIST THEORY

BY MARILYN FRYE

THE CROSSING PRESS / Trumansburg, New York 14886

The Crossing Press Feminist Series

Copyright © 1983 by Marilyn Frye

Cover design by Carol Terrizzi

Book design by Mary A. Scott

Typesetting by Martha J. Waters

Library of Congress Cataloging in Publication Data

Frye, Marilyn, 1941-
    The politics of reality.

    (The Crossing Press feminist series)
    1. Feminism--Addresses, essays, lectures.
I. Title. II. Series.
HQ1154.F78 1983 305.4'2   83-2082
ISBN 0-89594-100-7
ISBN 0-89594-099-X (pbk.)

CONTENTS

120781

PREFACE

The main themes of the first three essays in this collection
had taken shape by early 1974, as I began to teach a philosophy course on feminism. They have been central ever
since then to the course I have been teaching at Michigan
State University called "Philosophical Aspects of Feminism."
I want to dedicate this publication of "Oppression" to those
students for whom the experience of "the oppression lecture,"
at the beginning of that course, was something of a Rite of
Passage.

I began making notes toward a paper on separatism probably as early as 1970, but the connection between a politics
of separation (versus assimilation) and the kind of boundary-
drawing that is intrinsic to definition of words and concepts
grew slowly in my thoughts. The intuition and construction
of that connection was a significant part of the synthesis of
politics and philosophy without which I would have had to
abandon one or the other as meaningless. Since 1977 (during
which year I wrote "Some Reflections on Separatism and
Power") I have been exploring and clarifying for myself what
woman is in the phallocratic semantic systems of language,
myth and ritual and how that helps to explain and maintain
the political subordination (assimilation) of women. As will
be obvious to some readers, this work has been much informed by the work of other women, especially that of Ti-
Grace Atkinson, Mary Daly and Andrea Dworkin.

As a writer, I began in the academic environment where one prepares an essay and then goes before an audience and reads it aloud. Outside academia people sometimes hear speeches and sometimes encounter someone reading a story or a poem aloud to an audience, but the oral delivery of essays is not familiar. These essays are written at least as much for the ear as for the eye, perhaps more so; I hope they will be read aloud, both in and out of academic settings.

In most cases, the audience I imagined as I wrote was that provided by the Society for Women in Philosophy, usually the Midwestern Division. The women of that Society are a wonderful audience: attentive and excitable; critical; aesthetically sensitive, philosophically sophisticated and politically conscious; supportive, angry, stubborn, loving and logical. What more could a writer ask? . . .

Publication, love and money, of course.

At a time when it was just what I needed, Catherine Nicholson and Harriet Desmoines provided the perfect opportunity for publication with their well-named magazine, *Sinister Wisdom,* where they cheerfully published what was too feminist (not to mention too lesbian) for philosophy journals and too philosophical for lesbian feminist journals. Though I did not publish a great deal during their years of editorship, the existence of that magazine was vital to me, for it meant that whatever I was working on *could* be published. I am indebted to these women for their hearing me into speech.

Love. A writer could want the intelligent and knowledgeable collaboration, encouragement and criticism of a devoted friend and passionate lover. I have had that. And I will make sure she gets as much as she has given.

Money. I have made a decent living through these years at the sufferance of both women and men who have, in varying degrees at various times, yielded to the temptation to think me utterly mad, even dangerous, and have nonetheless not tried, at least not concertedly, to drive me out; of which I am glad. Some people in the institution in which I work have been kind, helpful, generous; some like me, some appreciate my work. I count all that among my blessings.

In addition to those already mentioned, the works of the following women have significantly and traceably influenced my own: Kathleen Barry, Michelle Cliff, Alix Dobkin, Susan Griffin, Sarah Hoagland, Susanne K. Langer, Kate Millett, Robin Morgan, Iris Murdoch, Catherine Nicholson, Adrienne Rich. Perhaps it is even more important to name some of the strong-willed women who have discussed and argued with me about matters vital to my work, both lovingly and in exasperation. First, Carolyn Shafer, with whom I have been as long as I have been with book, in whose erudition, thought, art and courage my work has many of its roots and by whose criticism it has been purged of many flaws. Others to whom I am grateful for their having the spirit for the risky conversations that are necessary to those who would go all the way include: Sandra Bartky, Claudia Card, Michelle Cliff, Harriet Desmoines, Reatha Fowler, Alison Jaggar, Catherine Madsen, Nellie McKay, Pat Michalek, Catherine Nicholson, Sandra Siegel, Regi Teasley, Sarah Thomson, Barrie Thorne, Eileen VanTassell, and many smart and stubborn women in my classes.

These essays are timebound and culturebound. Which should not need saying, perhaps, but does. The feminist thought and theory of college-educated white women has been far more accessible in print, so far, than that of women who have not enjoyed those privileges nor suffered the distinctive set of limitations that come with them; this work is undeniably part of that body of "white and college-educated" writing. It stands on those privileges and within those limits, as well as on and within the privileges and limits more particular to my own individual history and situation. To readers who might be able to overlook the ways in which my thought is limited by race- and classbound imagination: I have to ask you to take absolutely seriously both the warning and the invitation implicit in my occasional reminders that there exists a vast variety of women and women's lives which I know just enough about to point to but which I cannot speak from or for. To readers who could never overlook these limitations because of the insult to what you know: I not only invite your criticism but also ask that you use your own creativity and insight to make the best of mine, to carry out the translations and modifications which will make this work as useful to you as it can be.

Some have thought the limits of which I speak here are intrinsic to feminism itself. My life says that is not so. I have moved from an inexcusably innocent apolitical christian-styled liberalism toward the flexible wisdom of some sort of polylingual politics of variety. It is a fact of my biography that that progress began with and almost solely because of my engagement in the women's movement, and when courage or honor would fail, it is the logic of the feminism to which I am committed which compels my continued evolution. This feminism is in conception and intention a global politics; that is one of its greatest attractions and greatest promises. I and many others are growing into that politics, that promise. Growth is growth: sometimes there are things that can be done to hasten it, and sometimes it just has to be left alone. It is not always obvious what is best; one does what one can.

M.F.

INTRODUCTION

This work is a blend of philosophy and art. It is the partial articulation of a world view, of the shape and structure of the world as this philosopher knows it; it presents images and cameos which by reflections and associations suggest a larger story or picture of "how things are." The point of the undertaking is not to find and present "facts" (new or used), but to generate ways of conceiving and interpreting which illuminate the meanings of things already in some way known and to stimulate the invention of more new ways of thinking.

What I hope to illuminate is certainly not "already known" to everyone. Finally, of course, it is what is within my own ken and what I need and want to make sense of. What I take to be known will be taken for granted far more widely and readily among women than among men. Much of it is the data of women's experience, and much of it I learned from the feminist scholars and scientists who have made it their business to dis-cover, document and present "the facts" about women and the situations in which women live.

One of the great powers of feminism is that it goes so far in making the experiences and lives of women intelligible. Trying to make sense of one's own feelings, motivations, desires, ambitions, actions and reactions without taking into account the forces which maintain the subordination of women to men is like trying to explain why a marble stops rolling without taking friction into account. What "feminist theory" is about, to a great extent, is just identifying those forces (or some range of them or kinds of them) and displaying the mechanics of their applications to women as a group (or caste) and to individual women. The measure of the success of the theory is just how much sense it makes of what did not make sense before.

Developing theory of this sort is something like reading the varying patterns of the weather off a weathered landscape. The observations one makes on the ground are not used as data, in any strict sense of the word, so much as they give one *clues*. One proceeds more by something like an aesthetic sense of pattern or theme than by classical scientific method. Depending on what one has already figured out, a single detail of an anecdote from one woman's experience may be exactly as fertile a clue as a carefully gotten and fully documented statistical result of a study of a thousand women, and literature or a television sit-com may reflect the shape and velocity of the "prevailing winds" as intelligibly as real life.

The results of this theorizing are also something like charts of currents, trends and cycles of winds and storms, in that there is no implication that every single individual and item in the landscape is affected in just the same way by the same wind. One tree leans more than another: one may be more flexible, one may be more sheltered by other trees, one may be older, one may have been buffeted by both wind and flood. Similarly, the prevailing cultural wind that would cool women's anger to depression or freeze it into self-reproach does not have the same effect on every woman in every circumstance. A "prevailing wind" also is not absolutely constant. The trees by my house lean to the east because the prevailing winds come from the west. But they are not at every moment of every day suffering precisely that force from that direction. Sometimes there is no wind, and sometimes there is wind from the south. If "Women's anger is forbidden" is some sort of cultural truth, that would not imply that the force of that proscription is always and equally upon every individual in every situation.

None of us, in all our particularities, actually unfolds as a perfect print-out of the stereotypes of women that are promoted by the various segments of the culture. None of us is a perfect reflection even of the cultural forces we welcome or embrace, not to speak of those we deliberately resist. None of us obeys all the rules, even if we want to. But the stereotypes, the rules, the common expectations of us surround us all in a steady barrage of verbal and visual images in popular, elite, religious and underground vehicles of culture. Virtually every individual is immersed most of the time in a cultural medium which provides sexist and misogynist images of what we are and what we think we are doing. Our conceiving cannot be independent of culture, though it can be critical, resistant or rebellious. To the extent that an individual mother, for instance, does not mother in exact accord with advertising images of mothers, comic or religious images of mothers, racist images of mothers of her race, she is not independent of the power of those images but in tension with it. Her practice is affected by that tension.

Any theorist would be a fool to think she could tell another woman exactly how the particularities of that other woman's life reflect, or to what extent they do not reflect, the patterns the theorist has discerned. Even so, if it is true that women constitute something like a caste that cuts across divisions such as race and economic class, then although the forces which subordinate women would be modified, deflected and camouflaged in various ways by the other factors at play in our situations, we still ought to be able to describe those forces in ways which help make sense of the experiences of women who live in all sorts of different situations. I think this is possible, and I have aimed to do it. But finally, such illumination cannot be delivered complete and clear by one individual onto another's history and situation, not even if the two are very similar. If one person's theorizing is sound and correct enough to be useful to another, the other still has to make use of her own knowledge to transpose and interpret it, to adapt it to the details of her own life and circumstances, to make it her own.

A NOTE ON THE TEXT

The conventions for the uses of quotations marks and italics in this text will be familiar enough to professional philosophers, but others who are accustomed to texts prepared according to the *Modern Language Association Style Sheet* or other such standard authorities, and some readers who are unused to reading philosophical texts, may want some explanations.

I use *italics* for the titles of published books and periodicals, and enclose titles of articles, essays and short stories in quotation marks, as is called for in standard style guides. Foreign words appear in italics. Italics are otherwise used solely to indicate *emphasis;* when the essays are read aloud, italicized words and phrases should be stressed.

Quite frequently in these essays I have occasion to be talking about particular words, how they are used and what they mean. To do this, I have to have a device for referring to a word. It would be convenient for me if every word had a proper name, so I could refer to them by name: Tom, Martha, etc. But then I should have to introduce the reader to each word I expected to talk about, so s/he would know which name belonged to which word. That would not be convenient. The device I use is that of forming the name of a word by writing the letters of that word between two apostrophes. Thus:

The word 'spinster' has negative connotations to most speakers of English.

The word 'dyke' does not appear in most standard dictionaries.

The entire string of marks including both apostrophes functions in the sentence like a proper name would. Consequent-
ly, if the name of a word occurs at the end of a sentence or
phrase, the comma or period goes after the final apostrophe.
Thus:

> Mary Daly gave new life to the word 'spinster'.

I do not treat these apostrophes like quotation marks, since
what is going on when one refers to a word is not a quoting
of anyone or of any text. It is simply referring to a particular linguistic entity, and the apostrophes serve just as part of
the spelling of the name of that entity. It is more common
for preparers of texts to construct names of words by printing the words in italics. I do not do that because I do not
want references to words to be confused with emphasis or
stress.

Ordinary quotation marks are used here around titles of
articles and stories and also around words or phrases whose
usage I wish to indicate is questionable, odd or otherwise
remarkable:

> In "mental health" institutions, an angry woman is
> likely to be given electroshock "therapy."

Here, the quotation marks indicate that the expressions they
enclose are misleading, falsifying, inaccurate terms for the institutions and the processes they denote. I also use quotation
marks around terms I am using in a nonstandard way. In general, when a word or phrase appears in quotation marks, but
is not actually a direct quotation of some particular speaker
or author, the quotation marks are a signal that there is something fishy, phoney, nonstandard, anomalous or eccentric
about its usage, and the context will make clear in what way
and for what reason it is being set apart from the rest of the
text.

Finally, though my use of upper case letters is normal for the most part, I do not dignify names of religions and religious institutions with upper case letters. Hence, the word 'christian', used either as noun or as adjective, is not capitalized, nor is the word 'church' or 'catholic', etc. On the other hand, I do practice, from time to time, the deliberate reversal of standard typographical politics, and capitalize such words as 'Lesbian'. The occasional use of the plural pronouns 'they', 'them' and 'their' as singular pronouns where a singular and gender-neutral pronoun is needed is also deliberate, and should be chalked up to my politics, not to any weakness of my own or the editor's or proofreader's grasp of standard grammar. The usage of 'they', 'them' and 'their' as singular pronouns is very common in spoken English, and I view it as harmless in the written language.

OPPRESSION

It is a fundamental claim of feminism that women are oppressed. The word 'oppression' is a strong word. It repels and attracts. It is dangerous and dangerously fashionable and endangered. It is much misused, and sometimes not innocently.

The statement that women are oppressed is frequently met with the claim that men are oppressed too. We hear that oppressing is oppressive to those who oppress as well as to those they oppress. Some men cite as evidence of their oppression their much-advertised inability to cry. It is tough, we are told, to be masculine. When the stresses and frustrations of being a man are cited as evidence that oppressors are oppressed by their oppressing, the word 'oppression' is being stretched to meaninglessness; it is treated as though its scope includes any and all human experience of limitation or suffering, no matter the cause, degree or consequence. Once such usage has been put over on us, then if ever we deny that any person or group is oppressed, we seem to imply that we think they never suffer and have no feelings. We are accused of insensitivity; even of bigotry. For women, such accusation is particularly intimidating, since sensitivity is one of the few virtues that has been assigned to us. If we are found insensitive, we may fear we have no redeeming traits at all and perhaps are not real women. Thus are we silenced before we begin: the name of our situation drained of meaning and our guilt mechanisms tripped.

1

But this is nonsense. Human beings can be miserable without being oppressed, and it is perfectly consistent to deny that a person or group is oppressed without denying that they have feelings or that they suffer.

We need to think clearly about oppression, and there is much that mitigates against this. I do not want to undertake to prove that women are oppressed (or that men are not), but I want to make clear what is being said when we say it. We need this word, this concept, and we need it to be sharp and sure.

I

The root of the word 'oppression' is the element 'press'. *The press of the crowd; pressed into military service; to press a pair of pants; printing press; press the button.* Presses are used to mold things or flatten them or reduce them in bulk, sometimes to reduce them by squeezing out the gasses or liquids in them. Something pressed is something caught between or among forces and barriers which are so related to each other that jointly they restrain, restrict or prevent the thing's motion or mobility. Mold. Immobilize. Reduce.

The mundane experience of the oppressed provides another clue. One of the most characteristic and ubiquitous features of the world as experienced by oppressed people is the double bind—situations in which options are reduced to a very few and all of them expose one to penalty, censure or deprivation. For example, it is often a requirement upon oppressed people that we smile and be cheerful. If we comply, we signal our docility and our acquiescence in our situation. We need not, then, be taken note of. We acquiesce in being made invisible, in our occupying no space. We participate in our own erasure. On the other hand, anything but the sunniest countenance exposes us to being perceived as mean, bitter, angry or dangerous. This means, at the least, that we may be found "difficult" or unpleasant to work with, which is enough to cost one one's livelihood; at worst, being seen as mean, bitter, angry or dangerous has been known to result in rape, arrest, beating and murder. One can only choose to risk one's preferred form and rate of annihilation.

Another example: It is common in the United States that women, especially younger women, are in a bind where neither sexual activity nor sexual inactivity is all right. If she is heterosexually active, a woman is open to censure and punishment for being loose, unprincipled or a whore. The "punishment" comes in the form of criticism, snide and embarrassing remarks, being treated as an easy lay by men, scorn from her more restrained female friends. She may have to lie and hide her behavior from her parents. She must juggle the risks of unwanted pregnancy and dangerous contraceptives. On the other hand, if she refrains from heterosexual activity, she is fairly constantly harassed by men who try to persuade her into it and pressure her to "relax" and "let her hair down"; she is threatened with labels like "frigid," "uptight," "man-hater," "bitch" and "cocktease." The same parents who would be disapproving of her sexual activity may be worried by her inactivity because it suggests she is not or will not be popular, or is not sexually normal. She may be charged with lesbianism. If a woman is raped, then if she has been heterosexually active she is subject to the presumption that she liked it (since her activity is presumed to show that she likes sex), and if she has not been heterosexually active, she is subject to the presumption that she liked it (since she is supposedly "repressed and frustrated"). Both heterosexual activity and heterosexual nonactivity are likely to be taken as proof that you wanted to be raped, and hence, of course, weren't *really* raped at all. You can't win. You are caught in a bind, caught between systematically related pressures.

Women are caught like this, too, by networks of forces and barriers that expose one to penalty, loss or contempt whether one works outside the home or not, is on welfare or not, bears children or not, raises children or not, marries or not, stays married or not, is heterosexual, lesbian, both or

neither. Economic necessity; confinement to racial and/or
sexual job ghettos; sexual harassment; sex discrimination;
pressures of competing expectations and judgments about
women, wives and *mothers* (in the society at large, in racial
and ethnic subcultures and in one's own mind); dependence
(full or partial) on husbands, parents or the state; commitment to political ideas; loyalties to racial or ethnic or
other "minority" groups; the demands of self-respect and
responsibilities to others. Each of these factors exists in complex tension with every other, penalizing or prohibiting all of
the apparently available options. And nipping at one's heels,
always, is the endless pack of little things. If one dresses one
way, one is subject to the assumption that one is advertising
one's sexual availability; if one dresses another way, one
appears to "not care about oneself" or to be "unfeminine."
If one uses "strong language," one invites categorization as a
whore or slut; if one does not, one invites categorization as
a "lady"—one too delicately constituted to cope with robust
speech or the realities to which it presumably refers.

The experience of oppressed people is that the living of
one's life is confined and shaped by forces and barriers which
are not accidental or occasional and hence avoidable, but are
systematically related to each other in such a way as to catch
one between and among them and restrict or penalize motion
in any direction. It is the experience of being caged in: all
avenues, in every direction, are blocked or booby trapped.

Cages. Consider a birdcage. If you look very closely at
just one wire in the cage, you cannot see the other wires. If
your conception of what is before you is determined by this
myopic focus, you could look at that one wire, up and down
the length of it, and be unable to see why a bird would not
just fly around the wire any time it wanted to go somewhere.
Furthermore, even if, one day at a time, you myopically in-
spected each wire, you still could not see why a bird would
have trouble going past the wires to get anywhere. There is
no physical property of any one wire, *nothing* that the closest
scrutiny could discover, that will reveal how a bird could be

inhibited or harmed by it except in the most accidental way. It is only when you step back, stop looking at the wires one by one, microscopically, and take a macroscopic view of the whole cage, that you can see why the bird does not go anywhere; and then you will see it in a moment. It will require no great subtlety of mental powers. It is perfectly *obvious* that the bird is surrounded by a network of systematically related barriers, no one of which would be the least hindrance to its flight, but which, by their relations to each other, are as confining as the solid walls of a dungeon.

It is now possible to grasp one of the reasons why oppression can be hard to see and recognize: one can study the elements of an oppressive structure with great care and some good will without seeing the structure as a whole, and hence without seeing or being able to understand that one is looking at a cage and that there are people there who are caged, whose motion and mobility are restricted, whose lives are shaped and reduced.

The arresting of vision at a microscopic level yields such common confusion as that about the male door-opening ritual. This ritual, which is remarkably widespread across classes and races, puzzles many people, some of whom do and some of whom do not find it offensive. Look at the scene of the two people approaching a door. The male steps slightly ahead and opens the door. The male holds the door open while the female glides through. Then the male goes through. The door closes after them. "Now how," one innocently asks, "can those crazy womenslibbers say that is oppressive? The guy *removed* a barrier to the lady's smooth and unruffled progress." But each repetition of this ritual has a place in a pattern, in fact in several patterns. One has to shift the level of one's perception in order to see the whole picture.

The door-opening pretends to be a helpful service, but the helpfulness is false. This can be seen by noting that it will be done whether or not it makes any practical sense. Infirm men and men burdened with packages will open doors for able-bodied women who are free of physical burdens. Men will

impose themselves awkwardly and jostle everyone in order to
get to the door first. The act is not determined by convenience or grace. Furthermore, these very numerous acts of un-
needed or even noisome "help" occur in counterpoint to a
pattern of men not being helpful in many practical ways in
which women might welcome help. What *women* experience
is a world in which gallant princes charming commonly make
a fuss about being helpful and providing small services when
help and services are of little or no use, but in which there are
rarely ingenious and adroit princes at hand when substantial
assistance is really wanted either in mundane affairs or in situations of threat, assault or terror. There is no help with the
(his) laundry; no help typing a report at 4:00 a.m.; no help
in mediating disputes among relatives or children. There is
nothing but advice that women should stay indoors after
dark, be chaperoned by a man, or when it comes down to it,
"lie back and enjoy it."

The gallant gestures have no practical meaning. Their meaning is symbolic. The door-opening and similar services provided are services which really are needed by people who are
for one reason or another incapacitated—unwell, burdened
with parcels, etc. So the message is that women are incapable.
The detachment of the acts from the concrete realities of
what women need and do not need is a vehicle for the message that women's actual needs and interests are unimportant
or irrelevant. Finally, these gestures imitate the behavior of
servants toward masters and thus mock women, who are in
most respects the servants and caretakers of men. The message of the false helpfulness of male gallantry is female dependence, the invisibility or insignificance of women, and contempt for women.

One cannot see the meanings of these rituals if one's focus
is riveted upon the individual event in all its particularity, including the particularity of the individual man's present conscious intentions and motives and the individual woman's conscious perception of the event in the moment. It seems sometimes that people take a deliberately myopic view and fill

their eyes with things seen microscopically in order not to see macroscopically. At any rate, whether it is deliberate or not, people can and do fail to see the oppression of women be-cause they fail to see macroscopically and hence fail to see the various elements of the situation as systematically related in larger schemes.

As the cageness of the birdcage is a macroscopic phenom-enon, the oppressiveness of the situations in which women live our various and different lives is a macroscopic phenom-enon. Neither can be *seen* from a microscopic perspective. But when you look macroscopically you can see it—a network of forces and barriers which are systematically related and which conspire to the immobilization, reduction and molding of women and the lives we live.

II

The image of the cage helps convey one aspect of the systematic nature of oppression. Another is the selection of occupants of the cages, and analysis of this aspect also helps account for the invisibility of the oppression of women.

It is as a woman (or as a Chicana/o or as a Black or Asian or lesbian) that one is entrapped.

"Why can't I go to the park; you let Jimmy go!"
"Because it's not safe for girls."

"I want to be a secretary, not a seamstress; I don't want to learn to make dresses."

"There's no work for negroes in that line; learn a skill where you can earn your living."[1]

When you question why you are being blocked, why this bar-rier is in your path, the answer has not to do with individual talent or merit, handicap or failure; it has to do with your membership in some category understood as a "natural" or "physical" category. The "inhabitant" of the "cage" is not an individual but a group, all those of a certain category. If an individual is oppressed, it is in virtue of being a member of a group or category of people that is systematically reduced, molded, immobilized. Thus, to recognize a person as oppressed, one has to see that individual *as* belonging to a group of a certain sort.

There are many things which can encourage or inhibit perception of someone's membership in the sort of group or category in question here. In particular, it seems reasonable to suppose that if one of the devices of restriction and definition of the group is that of physical confinement or segregation, the confinement and separation would encourage recognition of the group as a group. This in turn would encourage the macroscopic focus which enables one to recognize oppression and encourages the individuals' identification and solidarity with other individuals of the group or category. But physical confinement and segregation of the group as a group is not common to all oppressive structures, and when an oppressed group is geographically and demographically dispersed the perception of it as a group is inhibited. There may be little or nothing in the situations of the individuals encouraging the macroscopic focus which would reveal the unity of the structure bearing down on all members of that group.*

A great many people, female and male and of every race and class, simply do not believe that *woman* is a category of oppressed people, and I think that this is in part because they have been fooled by the dispersal and assimilation of women throughout and into the systems of class and race which organize men. Our simply being dispersed makes it difficult for women to have knowledge of each other and hence difficult to recognize the shape of our common cage. The dispersal

---

* Coerced assimilation is in fact one of the *policies* available to an oppressing group in its effort to reduce and/or annihilate another group. This tactic is used by the U.S. government, for instance, on the American Indians.

and assimilation of women throughout economic classes and races also divides us against each other practically and economically and thus attaches *interest* to the inability to see: for some, jealousy of their benefits, and for some, resentment of the others' advantages.

To get past this, it helps to notice that in fact women of all races and classes *are* together in a ghetto of sorts. There is a women's place, a sector, which is inhabited by women of all classes and races, and it is not defined by geographical boundaries but by function. The function is the service of men and men's interests as men define them, which includes the bearing and rearing of children. The details of the service and the working conditions vary by race and class, for men of different races and classes have different interests, perceive their interests differently, and express their needs and demands in different rhetorics, dialects and languages. But there are also some constants.

Whether in lower, middle or upper-class home or work situations, women's service work always includes personal service (the work of maids, butlers, cooks, personal secretaries),* sexual service (including provision for his genital sexual needs and bearing his children, but also including "being nice," "being attractive for him," etc.), and ego service (encouragement, support, praise, attention). Women's service work also is characterized everywhere by the fatal combination of responsibility and powerlessness: we are held responsible and we hold ourselves responsible for good outcomes for men and children in almost every respect though we have in almost no case power adequate to that project. The details of the subjective experience of this servitude are local. They vary with economic class and race and ethnic tradition as well as the personalities of the men in question. So also are the details of the forces which coerce our tolerance of this servitude par-

---

* At higher class levels women may not *do* all these kinds of work, but are generally still responsible for hiring and supervising those who do it. These services are still, in these cases, women's responsibility.

ticular to the different situations in which different women live and work.

All this is not to say that women do not have, assert and manage sometimes to satisfy our own interests, nor to deny that in some cases and in some respects women's independent interests do overlap with men's. But at every race/class level and even across race/class lines men do not serve women as women serve men. "Women's sphere" may be understood as the "service sector," taking the latter expression much more widely and deeply than is usual in discussions of the economy.

III

It seems to be the human condition that in one degree or another we all suffer frustration and limitation, all encounter unwelcome barriers, and all are damaged and hurt in various ways. Since we are a social species, almost all of our behavior and activities are structured by more than individual inclination and the conditions of the planet and its atmosphere. No human is free of social structures, nor (perhaps) would happiness consist in such freedom. Structure consists of boundaries, limits and barriers; in a structured whole, some motions and changes are possible, and others are not. If one is looking for an excuse to dilute the word 'oppression', one can use the fact of social structure as an excuse and say that everyone is oppressed. But if one would rather get clear about what oppression is and is not, one needs to sort out the sufferings, harms and limitations and figure out which are elements of oppression and which are not.

From what I have already said here, it is clear that if one wants to determine whether a particular suffering, harm or limitation is part of someone's being oppressed, one has to look at it *in context* in order to tell whether it is an element in an oppressive structure: one has to see if it is part of an enclosing structure of forces and barriers which tends to the immobilization and reduction of a group or category of people. One has to look at how the barrier or force fits with others and to whose benefit or detriment it works. As soon as one looks at examples, it becomes obvious that not everything which frustrates or limits a person is oppressive, and not every harm or damage is due to or contributes to oppression.

If a rich white playboy who lives off income from his investments in South African diamond mines should break a leg in a skiing accident at Aspen and wait in pain in a blizzard for hours before he is rescued, we may assume that in that period he suffers. But the suffering comes to an end; his leg is repaired by the best surgeon money can buy and he is soon recuperating in a lavish suite, sipping Chivas Regal. Nothing in this picture suggests a structure of barriers and forces. He is a member of several oppressor groups and does not suddenly become oppressed because he is injured and in pain. Even if the accident was caused by someone's malicious negligence, and hence someone can be blamed for it and morally faulted, that person still has not been an agent of oppression.

Consider also the restriction of having to drive one's vehicle on a certain side of the road. There is no doubt that this restriction is almost unbearably frustrating at times, when one's lane is not moving and the other lane is clear. There are surely times, even, when abiding by this regulation would have harmful consequences. But the restriction is obviously wholesome for most of us most of the time. The restraint is imposed for our benefit, and does benefit us; its operation tends to encourage our *continued* motion, not to immobilize us. The limits imposed by traffic regulations are limits most of us would cheerfully impose on ourselves given that we knew others would follow them too. They are part of a structure which shapes our behavior, not to our reduction and immobilization, but rather to the protection of our continued ability to move and act as we will.

Another example: The boundaries of a racial ghetto in an American city serve to some extent to keep white people from going in, as well as to keep ghetto dwellers from going

out. A particular white citizen may be frustrated or feel deprived because s/he cannot stroll around there and enjoy the
"exotic" aura of a "foreign" culture, or shop for bargains in
the ghetto swap shops. In fact, the existence of the ghetto,
of racial segregation, does deprive the white person of knowledge and harm her/his character by nurturing unwarranted
feelings of superiority. But this does not make the white person in this situation a member of an oppressed race or a person oppressed because of her/his race. One must look at the
barrier. It limits the activities and the access of those on both
sides of it (though to different degrees). But it is a product of
the intention, planning and action of whites for the benefit of
whites, to secure and maintain privileges that are available to
whites generally, as members of the dominant and privileged
group. Though the existence of the barrier has some bad consequences for whites, the barrier does not exist in systematic
relationship with other barriers and forces forming a structure
oppressive to whites; quite the contrary. It is part of a structure which oppresses the ghetto dwellers and thereby (and by
white intention) protects and furthers white interests as dominant white culture understands them. This barrier is not oppressive to whites, even though it is a barrier to whites.

Barriers have different meanings to those on opposite sides
of them, even though they are barriers to both. The physical
walls of a prison no more dissolve to let an outsider in than to
let an insider out, but for the insider they are confining and
limiting while to the outsider they may mean protection from
what s/he takes to be threats posed by insiders—freedom from
harm or anxiety. A set of social and economic barriers and
forces separating two groups may be felt, even painfully, by
members of both groups and yet may mean confinement to
one and liberty and enlargement of opportunity to the other.

The service sector of the wives/mommas/assistants/girls is
almost exclusively a woman-only sector; its boundaries not
only enclose women but to a very great extent keep men out.
Some men sometimes encounter this barrier and experience
it as a restriction on their movements, their activities, their

control or their choices of "lifestyle." Thinking they might
like the simple nurturant life (which they may imagine to be
quite free of stress, alienation and hard work), and feeling deprived since it seems closed to them, they thereupon announce the discovery that they are oppressed, too, by "sex
roles." But that barrier is erected and maintained by men,
for the benefit of men. It consists of cultural and economic
forces and pressures in a culture and economy controlled by
men in which, at every economic level and in all racial and
ethnic subcultures, economy, tradition—and even ideologies
of liberation—work to keep at least local culture and economy
in male control.*

The boundary that sets apart women's sphere is maintained
and promoted by men generally for the benefit of men generally, and men generally do benefit from its existence, even
the man who bumps into it and complains of the inconveni-
ence. That barrier is protecting his classification and status
as a male, as superior, as having a right to sexual access to a
female or females. It protects a kind of citizenship which is
superior to that of females of his class and race, his access to
a wider range of better paying and higher status work, and
his right to prefer unemployment to the degradation of doing
lower status or "women's" work.

If a person's life or activity is affected by some force or
barrier that person encounters, one may not conclude that
the person is oppressed simply because the person encounters
that barrier or force; nor simply because the encounter is
unpleasant, frustrating or painful to that person at that time;
nor simply because the existence of the barrier or force, or
the processes which maintain or apply it, serve to deprive that

---

* Of course this is complicated by race and class. Machismo and
"Black manhood" politics seem to help keep Latin or Black men in
control of more cash than Latin or Black women control; but these
politics seem to me also to ultimately help keep the larger economy
in *white* male control.

person of something of value. One must look at the barrier
or force and answer certain questions about it. Who constructs and maintains it? Whose interests are served by its existence? Is it part of a structure which tends to confine, reduce and immobilize some group? Is the individual a member
of the confined group? Various forces, barriers and limitations a person may encounter or live with may be part of an
oppressive structure or not, and if they are, that person may
be on either the oppressed or the oppressor side of it. One
cannot tell which by how loudly or how little the person
complains.

IV

Many of the restrictions and limitations we live with are
more or less internalized and self-monitored, and are part of
our adaptations to the requirements and expectations imposed by the needs and tastes and tyrannies of others. I have
in mind such things as women's cramped postures and attenuated strides and men's restraint of emotional self-expression
(except for anger). Who gets what out of the practice of
those disciplines, and who imposes what penalties for improp-
er relaxations of them? What are the rewards of this self-
discipline?
  Can men cry? Yes, in the company of women. If a man
cannot cry, it is in the company of men that he cannot cry.
It is men, not women, who require this restraint; and men
not only require it, they reward it. The man who maintains
a steely or tough or laid-back demeanor (all are forms which
suggest invulnerability) marks himself as a member of the
male community and is esteemed by other men. Consequent-
ly, the maintenance of that demeanor contributes to the
man's self-esteem. It is felt as good, and he can feel good
about himself. The way this restriction fits into the structures
of men's lives is as one of the socially required behaviors
which, if carried off, contribute to their acceptance and re-

spect by significant others and to their own self-esteem. It is to their benefit to practice this discipline.

Consider, by comparison, the discipline of women's cramped physical postures and attenuated stride. This discipline can be relaxed in the company of women; it generally is at its most strenuous in the company of men.* Like men's emotional restraint, women's physical restraint is required by men. But unlike the case of men's emotional restraint, women's physical restraint is not rewarded. What do we get for it? Respect and esteem and acceptance? No. They mock us and parody our mincing steps. We look silly, incompetent, weak and generally contemptible. Our exercise of this discipline tends to low esteem and low self-esteem. It does not benefit us. It fits in a network of behaviors through which we constantly announce to others our membership in a lower caste and our unwillingness and/or inability to defend our bodily or moral integrity. It is degrading and part of a pattern of degradation.

Acceptable behavior for both groups, men and women, involves a required restraint that seems in itself silly and perhaps damaging. But the social effect is drastically different. The woman's restraint is part of a structure oppressive to women; the man's restraint is part of a structure oppressive to women.

V

One is marked for application of oppressive pressures by one's membership in some group or category. Much of one's suffering and frustration befalls one partly or largely because

---

* Cf., *Let's Take Back Our Space: "Female" and "Male" Body Language as a Result of Patriarchal Structures*, by Marianne Wex (Frauenliteratureverlag Hermine Fees, West Germany, 1979), especially p. 173. This remarkable book presents literally thousands of candid photographs of women and men, in public, seated, standing and lying down. It vividly demonstrates the very systematic differences in women's and men's postures and gestures.

one is a member of that category. In the case at hand, it is
the category, *woman*. Being a woman is a major factor in my
not having a better job than I do; being a woman selects me
as a likely victim of sexual assault or harassment; it is my being a woman that reduces the power of my anger to a proof
of my insanity. If a woman has little or no economic or political power, or achieves little of what she wants to achieve,
a major causal factor in this is that she is a woman. For any
woman of any race or economic class, being a woman is significantly attached to whatever disadvantages and depriva-
tions she suffers, be they great or small.

None of this is the case with respect to a person's being a
man. Simply being a man is not what stands between him
and a better job; whatever assaults and harassments he is
subject to, being male is not what selects him for victimization; being male is not a factor which would make his anger
impotent—quite the opposite. If a man has little or no material or political power, or achieves little of what he wants
to achieve, his being male is no part of the explanation. Being male is something he has going *for* him, even if race or
class or age or disability is going against him.

Women are oppressed, *as women*. Members of certain
racial and/or economic groups and classes, both the males
and the females, are oppressed *as* members of those races
and/or classes. But men are not oppressed *as men*.

   **. . . and isn't it strange that any of us should have been
confused and mystified about such a simple thing?**

NOTES

1. This example is derived from *Daddy Was A Number Runner*, by
Louise Meriwether (Prentice-Hall, Englewood Cliffs, New Jersey, 1970),
p. 144.

SEXISM

The first philosophical project I undertook as a feminist was that of trying to say carefully and persuasively what sexism is, and what it is for someone, some institution or some act to be sexist. This project was pressed on me with considerable urgency because, like most women coming to a feminist perception of themselves and the world, I was seeing sexism everywhere and trying to make it perceptible to others. I would point out, complain and criticize, but most frequently my friends and colleagues would not see that what I declared to be sexist was sexist, or at all objectionable.

As the critic and as the initiator of the topic, I was the one on whom the burden of proof fell—it was I who had to explain and convince. Teaching philosophy had already taught me that people cannot be persuaded of things they are not ready to be persuaded of; there are certain complexes of will and prior experience which will inevitably block persuasion, no matter the merits of the case presented. I knew that even if I could explain fully and clearly what I was saying when I called something sexist, I would not necessarily be able to convince various others of the correctness of this claim. But what troubled me enormously was that I could not explain it in any way which satisfied *me*. It is this sort of moral and intellectual frustration which, in my case at least, always generates philosophy.

The following was the product of my first attempt to state clearly and explicitly what sexism is:

> The term 'sexist' in its core and perhaps most fundamental meaning is a term which characterizes anything whatever which creates, constitutes, promotes or exploits any irrelevant or impertinent marking of the distinction between the sexes.[1]

When I composed this statement, I was thinking of the myriads of instances in which persons of the two sexes are treated differently, or behave differently, but where nothing in the real differences between females and males justifies or explains the difference of treatment or behavior. I was thinking, for instance, of the tracking of boys into Shop and girls into Home Ec, where one can see nothing about boys or girls considered in themselves which seems to connect essentially with the distinction between wrenches and eggbeaters. I was thinking also of sex discrimination in employment—cases where someone otherwise apparently qualified for a job is not hired because she is a woman. But when I tried to put this definition of 'sexist' to use, it did not stand the test.

Consider this case: If a company is hiring a supervisor who will supervise a group of male workers who have always worked for male supervisors, it can scarcely be denied that the sex of a candidate for the job is relevant to the candidate's prospects of moving smoothly and successfully into an effective working relationship with the supervisees (though the point is usually exaggerated by those looking for excuses not to hire women). Relevance is an intrasystematic thing. The patterns of behavior, attitude and custom within which a process goes on determine what is relevant to what in matters of describing, predicting or evaluating. In the case at hand, the workers' attitudes and the surrounding customs of the culture make a difference to how they interact with their supervisor and, in particular, *make* the sex of the supervisor a relevant factor in predicting how things will work out. So then, if the

company hires a man, in preference to a more experienced
and knowledgeable woman, can we explain our objection to
the decision by saying it involved distinguishing on the basis
of sex when sex is irrelevant to the ability to do the job? No:
sex is relevant here.

So, what did I mean to say about 'sexist'? I was thinking
that in a case of a candidate for a supervisory job, the reproductive capacity of the candidate has nothing to do with that
person's knowing what needs to be done and being able to
give properly timed, clear and correct directions. What I was
picturing was a situation purified of all sexist perception and
reaction. But, of course. *If* the whole context were not sexist, sex would not be an issue in such a job situation; indeed,
it might go entirely unnoticed. It is precisely the fact that the
sex of the candidate *is* relevant that is the salient symptom of
the sexism of the situation.

I had failed, in that first essay, fully to grasp or understand
that the locus of sexism is primarily in the system or framework, not in the particular act. It is not accurate to say that
what is going on in cases of sexism is that distinctions are
made on the basis of sex when sex is irrelevant; what is wrong
in cases of sexism is, in the first place, that sex *is* relevant;
and then that the making of distinctions on the basis of sex
reinforces the patterns which make it relevant.

In sexist cultural/economic systems, sex is always relevant.
To understand what sexism is, then, we have to step back and
take a larger view.

Sex-identification intrudes into every moment of our lives
and discourse, no matter what the supposedly primary focus
or topic of the moment is. Elaborate, systematic, ubiquitous
and redundant marking of a distinction between two sexes of
humans and most animals is customary and obligatory. One
never can ignore it.

Examples of sex-marking behavior patterns abound. A
couple enters a restaurant; the headwaiter or hostess addres-

ses the man and does not address the woman. The physician
addresses the man by surname and honorific (Mr. Baxter,
Rev. Jones) and addresses the woman by given name (Nancy,
Gloria). You congratulate your friend—a hug, a slap on the
back, shaking hands, kissing; one of the things which determines which of these you do is your friend's sex. In everything one does one has two complete repertoires of behavior,
one for interactions with women and one for interactions
with men. Greeting, storytelling, ordergiving and order-re-
ceiving, negotiating, gesturing deference or dominance, encouraging, challenging, asking for information: one does all
of these things differently depending upon whether the relevant others are male or female.

That this is so has been confirmed in sociological and
socio-linguistic research,[2] but it is just as easily confirmed in
one's own experience. To discover the differences in how
you greet a woman and how you greet a man, for instance,
just observe yourself, paying attention to the following sorts
of things: frequency and duration of eye contact, frequency
and type of touch, tone and pitch of voice, physical distance
maintained between bodies, how and whether you smile, use
of slang or swear words, whether your body dips into a sha-
dow curtsy or bow. That I have two repertoires for handling
introductions to people was vividly confirmed for me when a
student introduced me to his friend, Pat, and I really could
not tell what sex Pat was. For a moment I was stopped
cold, completely incapable of action. I felt myself helpless-
ly caught between two paths—the one I would take if Pat
were female and the one I would take if Pat were male.
Of course the paralysis does not last. One is rescued by one's
ingenuity and good will; one can invent a way to behave as
one says "How do you do?" to a human being. But the habitual ways are not for humans: they are one way for women
and another for men.

Interlaced through all our behavior is our speaking—our
linguistic behavior. Third person singular pronouns mark the
sex of their referents. The same is true for a huge range of

the nouns we use to refer to people ('guy', 'boy', 'lady', 'salesman', etc., and all the terms which covertly indicate the sex of the referent, like 'pilot', 'nurse', etc.), and the majority of given proper names ('Bob', 'Gwen', etc.).* In speaking, one constantly marks the sexes of those one speaks about.

The frequency with which our behavior marks the sexes of those we interact with cannot be exaggerated. The phenomenon is absolutely pervasive and deeply entrenched in all the patterns of behavior which are habitual, customary, acceptable, tolerable and intelligible. One can invent ways of behaving in one situation or another which are not sex-marking, which do not vary with the sexes of the persons involved, but if one were to succeed in removing sex-marking from one's behavior altogether, one's behavior would be so odd as to precipitate immediate crises of intelligibility and strenuous moral, religious or aesthetic objections from others. Everything one did would seem strange. And this is a matter of no small moment. We are a gregarious species. Our lives depend on our abilities to interact with others in relations of work, of exchange and of sympathy. What one cannot do without seeming excessively odd or unintelligible, one cannot do without severe disturbance to patterns of interaction upon which one's life depends. Sex-marking behavior is not optional; it is as obligatory as it is pervasive.

---

* Languages differ in their degree of "gender-loading" and there is evidence that these differences correlate with differences in the ages at which children "attain gender identity." In "Native Language and Cognitive Structures—A Cross-cultural Inquiry," Alexander Z. Guiora and Arthur Herold detail this evidence. They characterize English as having "minimal" gender-loading, Hebrew as having "maximum gender-loading" and Finnish as having "zero." If English, whose gender-marking seems so very prevalent to me, is an example of "minimal gender-loading," it seems safe to assume that gender-marking in human languages is indeed a significant factor in human experience generally. (The Guiora and Herold article may be requested from Dr. Guiora at Box No. 011, University Hospital, The University of Michigan, Ann Arbor, Michigan 48109.) I am indebted to Barbara Abbott for bringing this article to my attention.

Closely connected with habitual and obligatory sex-marking is a constant and urgent need to know or be able to guess the sex of every single person with whom one has the slightest or most remote contact or interaction. If we are going to mark people's sexes in every situation, then we have to know their sexes. I needed to know whether "Pat" was endowed with a clitoris or a penis prior to making the first step in getting acquainted. If I am writing a book review, the use of personal pronouns to refer to the author creates the need to know whether that person's reproductive cells are the sort which produce ova or the sort which produce sperm. I cannot ask the time of day without first knowing or presuming I know my informant's potential role in reproduction. We are socially and communicatively helpless if we do not know the sex of everybody we have anything to do with, and for members of such a species as ours, such helplessness can be life-threatening. Our habitual behavior patterns make knowledge of each person's sex both pervasively pertinent and of the *first* importance. Furthermore, the importance and urgency of having such knowledge is intensified by another sort of factor which I think most people rarely notice because they *do* usually know the sexes of others.

In a culture in which one is deemed sinful, sick or disgusting (at least) if one is not heterosexual, it is very important to keep track of one's sexual feelings and the sexes of those who inspire them. If one is permitted sexual expression or gratification, or even mere feeling, with persons of one sex but not of the other, one has to know what sex each person is before one can allow one's heart to beat or one's blood to flow in erotic enjoyment of that person. Much of our ordinary and apparently nonsexual interaction and communication involves elements of sexual or erotic message, and these are *rigidly* regulated by sex taboos, including the taboo on homosexuality. The adjustment or maladjustment of these messages to the sex of the person in question can have wonderful or disastrous consequences. The thought that one might misapprehend the sex of another conjures nothing less than the holy dread of unwitting violation of powerful taboo.   Thus all the tension connected with sexual taboo and repression intensifies the urgency of being acceptable and intelligible, and our need to know everyone's sex carries much of the weight of an acute and emotionally fraught survival need.

The pressure on each of us to guess or determine the sex of everybody else both generates and is exhibited in a great pressure on each of us to *inform* everybody all the time of our sex.   For, if you strip humans of most of their cultural trappings, it is not always that easy to tell without close inspection which are female, which are male.   The tangible and visible physical differences between the sexes are not particularly sharp or numerous.   Individual variation along the physical dimensions we think of as associated with maleness and femaleness are great, and the differences between the sexes could easily be obscured by bodily decoration, hair removal and the like.   One of the shocks, when one does mistake someone's sex, is the discovery of how easily one can be misled.   We could not ensure that we could identify people by their sex virtually any time and anywhere under any conditions if they did not announce themselves, did not *tell* us in one way or another.

We do not, in fact, announce our sexes "in one way or another."   We announce them in a thousand ways.   We deck ourselves from head to toe with garments and decorations which serve like badges and buttons to announce our sexes. For every type of occasion there are distinct clothes, gear and accessories, hairdos, cosmetics and scents, labeled as "ladies' " or "men's" and labeling us as females or males, and most of the time most of us choose, use, wear or bear the paraphernalia associated with our sex.   It goes below the skin as well. There are different styles of gait, gesture, posture, speech, humor, taste and even of perception, interest and attention that we learn as we grow up to be women or to be men and that label and announce us as women or as men. It begins early in life: even infants in arms are color coded.

That we wear and bear signs of our sexes, and that this is compulsory, is made clearest in the relatively rare cases when we do not do so, or not enough. Responses ranging from critical to indignant to hostile meet mothers whose small children are not immediately sex-identifiable, and hippies used to be accosted on the streets (by otherwise reserved and polite people) with criticisms and accusations when their clothing and style gave off mixed and contradictory sex-announcements. Anyone in any kind of job placement service and any Success Manual will tell you that you cannot expect to get or keep a job if your clothing or personal style is ambiguous in its announcement of your sex. You don't go to a job interview wearing the other sex's shoes and socks.

The buzz on this last example indicates another source of pressure to inform each other of our sexes, namely, once again, the requirement that one be and appear heterosexual. Queerly enough, one appears heterosexual by informing people of one's sex *very* emphatically and *very* unambiguously, and one does this by heaping into one's behavior and upon one's body ever more and more conclusive sex-indicators. For homosexuals and lesbians who wish to pass as heterosexual, it is these indicators that provide most of the camouflage; for those who wish to avoid being presumed heterosexual, the trick is to deliberately cultivate ambiguous sex-indicators in clothes, behavior and style. In a culture in which homosexuality and lesbianism are violently and almost universally forbidden, and heterosexuality is announced by announcing one's sex, it always behooves one to announce one's sex.

The information as to what sex one is is always wanted, and supplying it is always appropriate to one's own and others' most constant and pervasive interests—interests in being and remaining viable in the available human community.

The intense demand for marking and for asserting what sex each person is adds up to a strenuous requirement that there *be* two distinct and sharply dimorphic sexes. But, in reality, there are not. There are people who fit on a biological spectrum between two not-so-sharply defined poles. In about 5 percent of live births, possibly more, the babies are in some degree and way not perfect exemplars of male and female. There are individuals with chromosome patterns other than XX or XY and individuals whose external genitalia at birth exhibit some degree of ambiguity. There are people who are chromosomally "normal" who are at the far ends of the normal spectra of secondary sex characteristics—height, musculature, hairiness, body density, distribution of fat, breast size, etc.—whose overall appearance fits the norm of people whose chromosomal sex is the opposite of theirs.[3]

These variations not withstanding, persons (mainly men, of course) with the power to do so actually *construct* a world in which men are men and women are women and there is nothing in between and nothing ambiguous; they do it by chemically and/or surgically altering people whose bodies are indeterminate or ambiguous with respect to sex. Newborns with "imperfectly formed" genitals are immediately "corrected" by chemical or surgical means, children and adolescents are given hormone "therapies" if their bodies seem not to be developing according to what physicians and others declare to be the norm for what has been declared to be that individual's sex. Persons with authority recommend and supply cosmetics and cosmetic regimens, diets, exercises and all manner of clothing to revise or disguise the too-hairy lip, the too-large breast, the too-slender shoulders, the too-large feet, the too-great or too-slight stature. Individuals whose bodies do not fit the picture of exactly two sharply dimorphic sexes are often enough quite willing to be altered or veiled for the obvious reason that the world punishes them severely for their failure to be the "facts" which would verify the doctrine of two sexes. The demand that the world be a world in which there are exactly two sexes is inexorable, and we are all com-

pelled to answer to it emphatically, unconditionally, repeti-
tiously and unambiguously.

Even being physically "normal" for one's assigned sex is
not enough. One must *be* female or male, actively. Again,
the costumes and performances. Pressed to acting feminine
or masculine, one colludes (co-lude: play along) with the
doctors and counselors in the creation of a world in which
the apparent dimorphism of the sexes is so extreme that one
can only think there is a great gulf between female and male,
that the two are, essentially and fundamentally and naturally,
utterly different. One helps to create a world in which it
seems to us that we *could* never mistake a woman for a man
or a man for a woman. We never need worry.

Along with all the making, marking and announcing of sex-
distinction goes a strong and visceral feeling or attitude to the
effect that sex-distinction is the most important thing in the
world: that it would be the end of the world if it were not
maintained, clear and sharp and rigid; that a sex-dualism
which is rooted in the nature of the beast is absolutely crucial
and fundamental to all aspects of human life, human society
and human economy. Where feminism is perceived as a project of blurring this distinction, antifeminist rhetoric is vivid
with the dread that the world will end if the feminists have
their way.[4] Some feminists' insistence that the feminist goal
is *not* a "unisex" society is defensive in a way that suggests
they too believe that culture or civilization would not survive
blurring the distinction. I think that one of the sources of the
prevalence and profundity of this conviction and dread is our
immersion in the very behavior patterns I have been discussing.

It is a general and obvious principle of information theory
that when it is very, very important that certain information
be conveyed, the suitable strategy is redundancy. If a message
must get through, one sends it repeatedly and by as many
means or media as one has at one's command. On the other
end, as a receiver of information, if one receives the same in-

formation over and over, conveyed by every medium one knows, another message comes through as well, and implicitly: the message that this information is very, very important. The enormous frequency with which information about people's sexes is conveyed conveys implicitly the message that this topic is enormously important. I suspect that this is the single topic on which we most frequently receive information from others throughout our entire lives. If I am right, it would go part way to explaining why we end up with an almost irresistible impression, unarticulated, that the matter of people's sexes is the most important and most fundamental topic in the world.

We exchange sex-identification information, along with the implicit message that it is very important, in a variety of circumstances in which there really is no concrete or experientially obvious point in having the information. There are reasons, as this discussion has shown, why you should want to know whether the person filling your water glass or your tooth is male or female and why that person wants to know what you are, but those reasons are woven invisibly into the fabric of social structure and they do not have to do with the bare mechanics of things being filled. Furthermore, the same culture which drives us to this constant information exchange also simultaneously enforces a strong blanket rule requiring that the simplest and most nearly definitive physical manifestations of sex difference be hidden from view in all but the most private and intimate circumstances. The double message of sex-distinction and its pre-eminent importance is conveyed, in fact, in part *by* devices which systematically and deliberately cover up and hide from view the few physical things which do (to a fair extent) distinguish two sexes of humans. The messages are overwhelmingly dissociated from the concrete facts they supposedly pertain to, and from matrices of concrete and sensible reasons and consequences.

Small children's minds must be hopelessly boggled by all this. We know our own sexes, and learn to think it a matter of first importance that one is a girl or a boy so early that we do not remember not knowing—long before physical differences in our young bodies could make more than the most trivial practical differences. A friend of mine whose appearance and style have a little bit about them that is gender-ambiguous walked past a mother and child, and heard the child ask the mother, "Is she a man or a woman?" The struggle to divine some connection between social behavior and physical sex, and the high priority of it all, seem painfully obvious here.

If one is made to feel that a thing is of prime importance, but common sensory experience does not connect it with things of obvious concrete and practical importance, then there is mystery, and with that a strong tendency to the construction of mystical or metaphysical conceptions of its importance. If it is important, but not of mundane importance, it must be of transcendent importance. All the more so if it is *very* important.*

This matter of our sexes must be very profound indeed if it must, on pain of shame and ostracism, be covered up and must, on pain of shame and ostracism, be boldly advertised by every means and medium one can devise.

There is one more point about redundancy that is worth making here. If there is one thing more effective in making one believe a thing than receiving the message repetitively, it is rehearsing it repetitively. Advertisers, preachers, teachers, all of us in the brainwashing professions, make use of this apparently physical fact of human psychology routinely. The

---

* For some readers it will be useful to note a connection here with H.P. Grice's doctrine of conversational implicatures. There is a conversational "rule" to the effect that a speaker should "be relevant." As audiences we assume information given us is relevant, and if we cannot see its relevance we generally assume the relevance is to something hidden or that we are somehow missing something others see; or we invent a relevance by reconstruing the information as about something other than it initially appeared to be about. (Grice, "Logic and Conversation," *The Logic of Grammar*, edited by Donald Davidson and Gilbert Harman [Dickenson Publishing Company, Inc., Encino, California and Belmont, California, 1975], pp. 64-75.)

redundancy of sex-marking and sex-announcing serves not only to make the topic seem transcendently important, but to make the sex-duality it advertises seem transcendently and unquestionably *true*.

It is quite a spectacle, really, once one sees it, these humans so devoted to dressing up and acting out and "fixing" one another so everyone lives up to and lives out the theory that there are two sharply distinct sexes and never the twain shall overlap or be confused or conflated; these hominids constantly and with remarkable lack of embarrassment marking a distinction between two sexes as though their lives depended on it. It is wonderful that homosexuals and lesbians are mocked and judged for "playing butch-femme roles" and for dressing in "butch-femme drag," for nobody goes about in full public view as thoroughly decked out in butch and femme drag as respectable heterosexuals when they are dressed up to go out in the evening, or to go to church, or to go to the office. Heterosexual critics of queers' "role-playing" ought to look at themselves in the mirror on their way out for a night on the town to see who's in drag. The answer is, everybody is. Perhaps the main difference between heterosexuals and queers is that when queers go forth in drag, they know they are engaged in theater—they are playing and they know they are playing. Heterosexuals usually are taking it all perfectly seriously, thinking they are in the real world, thinking they *are* the real world.

Of course, in a way, they are the real world. All this bizarre behavior has a function in the construction of the real world.

Sex-marking and sex-announcing are equally compulsory for males and females; but that is as far as equality goes in this matter. The meaning and import of this behavior is profoundly different for women and for men.

Imagine. . .

A colony of humans established a civilization hundreds of years ago on a distant planet. It has evolved, as civilizations will. Its language is a descendant of English.

The language has personal pronouns marking the child/adult distinction, and its adult personal pronouns mark the distinction between straight and curly pubic hair. At puberty each person assumes distinguishing clothing styles and manners so others can tell what type she or he is without the closer scrutiny which would generally be considered indecent. People with straight pubic hair adopt a style which is modest and self-effacing and clothes which are fragile and confining; people with curly pubic hair adopt a style which is expansive and prepossessing and clothes which are sturdy and comfortable. People whose pubic hair is neither clearly straight nor clearly curly alter their hair chemically in order to be clearly one or the other. Since those with curly pubic hair have higher status and economic advantages, those with ambiguous pubic hair are told to make it straight, for life will be easier for a low-status person whose category might be doubted than for a high-status person whose category might be doubted.

It is taboo to eat or drink in the same room with any person of the same pubic hair type as oneself. Compulsory heterogourmandism, it is called by social critics, though most people think it is just natural human desire to eat with one's pubic-hair opposite. A logical consequence of this habit, or taboo, is the limitation to dining only singly or in pairs—a taboo against banquetism, or, as the slang expression goes, against the group gulp.

Whatever features an individual male person has which tend to his social and economic disadvantage (his age, race, class, height, etc.), one feature which never tends to his disadvantage in the society at large is his maleness. The case for females is the mirror image of this. Whatever features an individual female person has which tend to her social and economic advantage (her age, race, etc.), one feature which always tends to her disadvantage is her femaleness. Therefore, when a male's sex-category is the thing about him that gets first and most repeated notice, the thing about him that is being framed and emphasized and given primacy is a feature which in general is an asset to him. When a female's sex-category is the thing about her that gets first and most repeated notice, the thing about her that is being framed and emphasized and given primacy is a feature which in general is a liability to her. Manifestations of this divergence in the meaning and consequences of sex-announcement can be very concrete.

Walking down the street in the evening in a town or city exposes one to some risk of assault. For males the risk is less; for females the risk is greater. If one announces oneself male, one is presumed by potential assailants to be more rather than less likely to defend oneself or be able to evade the assault and, if the male-announcement is strong and unambiguous, to be a noncandidate for sexual assault. If one announces oneself female, one is presumed by potential assailants to be less rather than more likely to defend oneself or to evade the assault and, if the female-announcement is strong and unambiguous, to be a prime candidate for sexual assault. Both the man and the woman "announce" their sex through style of gait, clothing, hair style, etc., but they are not equally or identically affected by announcing their sex. The male's announcement tends toward his protection or safety, and the female's announcement tends toward her victimization. It could not be more immediate or concrete; the meaning of the sex-identification could not be more different.

The sex-marking behavioral repertoires are such that in the behavior of almost all people of both sexes addressing or responding to males (especially within their own culture/race) generally is done in a manner which suggests basic respect, while addressing or responding to females is done in a manner that suggests the females' inferiority (condescending tones, presumptions of ignorance, overfamiliarity, sexual aggression, etc.). So, when one approaches an ordinary well-socialized person in such cultures, if one is male, one's own behavioral announcement of maleness tends to evoke supportive and beneficial response and if one is female, one's own behavioral announcement of femaleness tends to evoke degrading and detrimental response.

The details of the sex-announcing behaviors also contribute to the reduction of women and the elevation of men. The case is most obvious in the matter of clothing. As feminists have been saying for two hundred years or so, ladies' clothing is generally restrictive, binding, burdening and frail; it threatens to fall apart and/or to uncover something that is supposed to be covered if you bend, reach, kick, punch or run. It typically does not protect effectively against hazards in the environment, nor permit the wearer to protect herself against the hazards of the human environment. Men's clothing is generally the opposite of all this—sturdy, suitably protective, permitting movement and locomotion. The details of feminine manners and postures also serve to bind and restrict. To be feminine is to take up little space, to defer to others, to be silent or affirming of others, etc. It is not necessary here to survey all this, for it has been done many times and in illuminating detail in feminist writings. My point here is that though both men and women must behave in sex-announcing ways, the behavior which announces femaleness is in itself both physically and socially binding and limiting as the behavior which announces maleness is not.

The sex-correlated variations in our behavior tend systematically to the benefit of males and the detriment of females. The male, announcing his sex in sex-identifying behavior and dress, is both announcing and acting on his membership in a dominant caste—dominant within his subculture and to a fair

extent across subcultures as well. The female, announcing her
sex, is both announcing and acting on her membership in the
subordinated caste. She is obliged to inform others constantly and in every sort of situation that she is to be treated as inferior, without authority, assaultable. She cannot move or
speak within the usual cultural norms without engaging in
self-deprecation. The male cannot move or speak without engaging in self-aggrandizement. Constant sex-identification
both defines and maintains the caste boundary without which
there could not be a dominance-subordination structure.

The forces which make us mark and announce sexes are
among the forces which constitute the oppression of women,
and they are central and essential to the maintenance of that
system.

Oppression is a system of interrelated barriers and forces
which reduce, immobilize and mold people who belong to a
certain group, and effect their subordination to another group
(individually to individuals of the other group, and as a group,
to that group). Such a system could not exist were not the
groups, the categories of persons, well defined. Logically, it
presupposes that there are two distinct categories. Practically, they must be not only distinct but relatively easily identi-
fiable; the barriers and forces could not be suitably located
and applied if there were often much doubt as to which individuals were to be contained and reduced, which were to dom-
inate.[5]

It is extremely costly to subordinate a large group of people simply by applications of material force, as is indicated by
the costs of maximum security prisons and of military supres-
sion of nationalist movements. For subordination to be per-
manent and cost effective, it is necessary to create conditions
such that the subordinated group acquiesces to some extent
in the subordination. Probably one of the most efficient ways
to secure acquiescence is to convince the people that their
subordination is inevitable. The mechanisms by which the

subordinate and dominant categories are defined can contribute greatly to popular belief in the inevitability of the dominance/subordination structure.

For efficient subordination, what's wanted is that the structure not appear to be a cultural artifact kept in place by human decision or custom, but that it appear *natural*—that it appear to be a quite direct consequence of facts about the beast which are beyond the scope of human manipulation or revision. It must seem natural that individuals of the one category are dominated by individuals of the other and that as groups, the one dominates the other.[6] To make this seem natural, it will help if it seems to all concerned that members of the two groups are *very* different from each other, and this appearance is enhanced if it can be made to appear that within each group, the members are very like one another. In other words, the appearance of the naturalness of the dominance of men and the subordination of women is supported by anything which supports the appearance that men are very like other men and very unlike women, and that women are very like other women and very unlike men. All behavior which encourages the appearance that humans are biologically sharply sex-dimorphic encourages the acquiescence of women (and, to the extent it needs encouragement, of men) in women's subordination.

That we are trained to behave so differently as women and as men, and to behave so differently toward women and toward men, itself contributes mightily to the appearance of extreme natural dimorphism, but also, the *ways* we act as women and as men, and the *ways* we act toward women and toward men, mold our bodies and our minds to the shapes of subordination and dominance. We do become what we practice being.

Throughout this essay I have seemed to beg the question at hand. Should I not be trying to prove that there are few and insignificant differences between females and males, if that is what I believe, rather than assuming it? What I have been doing is offering observations which suggest that if one thinks there are biologically deep differences between women and men which cause and justify divisions of labor and responsibility such as we see in the modern patriarchal family and male-dominated workplace, one may *not* have arrived at this belief because of direct experience of unmolested physical evidence, but because our customs serve to construct that appearance; and I suggest that these customs are artifacts of culture which exist to support a morally and scientifically insupportable system of dominance and subordination.[7]

But also, in the end, I do not want to claim simply that there are not socially significant biologically-grounded differences between human females and males. Things are much more complex than that.

Enculturation and socialization are, I think, misunderstood if one pictures them as processes which apply layers of cultural gloss over a biological substratum. It is with that picture in mind that one asks whether this or that aspect of behavior is due to "nature" or "nurture." One means, does it emanate from the biological substratum or does it come from some layer of the shellac? A variant on this wrong picture is the picture according to which enculturation or socialization is something mental or psychological, as opposed to something physical or biological. Then one can think of attitudes and habits of perception, for instance, as "learned" versus "biologically determined." And again, one can ask such things as whether men's aggressiveness is learned or biologically determined, and if the former is asserted, one can think in terms of changing them while if the latter is asserted, one must give up all thought of reform.

My observations and experience suggest another way of looking at this. I see enormous social pressure on us all to act feminine or act masculine (and not both), so I am inclined to think that if we were to break the habits of culture which generate that pressure, people would not act particularly masculine or feminine. The fact that there are such penalties threatened for deviations from these patterns strongly suggests that the patterns would not be there but for the threats. This leads, I think, to a skeptical conclusion: we do not know whether human behavior patterns would be dimorphic along lines of chromosomal sex if we were not threatened and bullied; nor do we know, if we assume that they would be dimorphous, *what* they would be, that is, *what* constellations of traits and tendencies would fall out along that genetic line. And these questions are odd anyway, for there is no question of humans growing up *without* culture, so we don't know what other cultural variables we might imagine to be at work in a culture in which the familiar training to masculinity and femininity were not going on.

On the other hand, as one goes about in the world, and in particular as one tries out strategies meant to alter the behaviors which constitute and support male dominance, one often has extremely convincing experiences of the *inflexibility* of people in this respect, of a resistance to change which seems to run much, much deeper than willingness or willfulness in the face of arguments and evidence. As feminist activists, many of us have felt this most particularly in the case of men, and it has sometimes seemed that the relative flexibility and adaptability of women and the relative rigidity of men are so widespread within each group respectively, and so often and convincingly encountered, that they must be biologically given. And one watches men and women on the streets, and their bodies seem so different—one hardly can avoid thinking there are vast and profound differences between women and men without giving up the hard won confidence in one's powers of perception.

The first remedy here is to lift one's eyes from a single culture, class and race. If the bodies of Asian women set them apart so sharply from Asian men, see how different they are also from Black women; if white men all look alike and very different from white women, it helps to note that Black men don't look so like white men.

The second remedy is to think about the subjective experience we have of our *habits*. If one habitually twists a lock of one's hair whenever one is reading and has tried to break this habit, one knows how "bodily" it is; but that does not convince one it is genetically determined. People who drive to work every day often take the same route every day, and if they mean to take another route one day in order to do an errand on the way, they may find themselves at work, conveyed along the habitual route, without having revised the decision to do the errand. The habit of taking that course is mapped into one's body; it is not a matter of a decision—a mental event—that is repeated each day upon a daily re-judgment of the reasonableness of the course. It is also not genetic. We are animals. Learning is physical, bodily. There is not a separate, nonmaterial "control room" where socialization, enculturation and habit formation take place and where, since it is nonmaterial, change is independent of bodies and easier than in bodies.

Socialization molds our bodies; enculturation forms our skeletons, our musculature, our central nervous systems. By the time we are gendered adults, masculinity and femininity *are* "biological." They are structural and material features of how our bodies are. My experience suggests that they are changeable just as one would expect bodies to be—slowly, through constant practice and deliberate regimens designed to remap and rebuild nerve and tissue. This is how many of us *have* changed when we chose to change from "women" as culturally defined to "women" as we define ourselves. Both the sources of the changes and the resistances to them are bodily—are among the possibilities of our animal natures, whatever those may be.

But now "biological" does not mean "genetically determined" or "inevitable." It just means "of the animal."

It is no accident that feminism has often focused on our bodies. Rape, battering, reproductive self-determination, health, nutrition, self-defense, athletics, financial independence (control of the means of feeding and sheltering ourselves). And it is no accident that with varying degrees of conscious intention, feminists have tried to create separate spaces where women could exist somewhat sheltered from the prevailing winds of patriarchal culture and try to stand up straight for once. One needs space to *practice* an erect posture; one cannot just will it to happen. To retrain one's body one needs physical freedom from what are, in the last analysis, physical forces misshaping it to the contours of the subordinate.

The cultural and economic structures which create and enforce elaborate and rigid patterns of sex-marking and sexannouncing behavior, that is, create gender as we know it, mold us as dominators and subordinates (I do not say "mold our minds" or "mold our personalities"). They construct two classes of animals, the masculine and the feminine, where another constellation of forces might have constructed three or five categories, and not necessarily hierarchically related. Or such a spectrum of sorts that we would not experience them as "sorts" at all.

The term 'sexist' characterizes cultural and economic structures which create and enforce the elaborate and rigid patterns of sex-marking and sex-announcing which divide the species, along lines of sex, into dominators and subordinates. Individual acts and practices are sexist which reinforce and support those structures, either as culture or as shapes taken on by the enculturated animals. Resistance to sexism is that which undermines those structures by social and political action and by projects of reconstruction and revision of ourselves.

NOTES

1. "Male Chauvinism—A Conceptual Analysis," *Philosophy and Sex,* edited by Robert Baker and Frederick Elliston (Prometheus Books, Buffalo, New York, 1975), p. 66. The inadequacies of such an account of sexism are reflected in the inadequacies of a standard legal interpretation of what sex discrimination is as it is analyzed by Catharine A. MacKinnon in *Sexual Harassment of Working Women* (Yale University Press, New Haven and London, 1979), cf. Chapters 5 and 6. See also my review of this book, "Courting Gender Justice," *New Women's Times Feminist Review,* No. 17, September-October 1981, pp. 10-11.

2. See, for example, such works as *Body Politics: Power, Sex and Nonverbal Communication,* by Nancy Henley (Prentice-Hall, Englewood Cliffs, New Jersey, 1977); *Language and Sex: Difference and Dominance,* edited by Barrie Thorne and Nancy Henley (Newbury House Publishers, Rowley, Massachusetts, 1975); and *Gender and Nonverbal Behavior,* edited by Clara Mayo and Nancy M. Henley (Springer-Verlag, New York, 1981).

3. I rely here on lectures by Eileen Van Tassell in which she interpreted the generally available data on sex-characteristics, sex-differences and sex-similarities. One can refer, in particular, to *Man and Woman, Boy and Girl,* by John Money and Anke A. Ehrhardt (The Johns Hopkins University Press, 1972) and *Intersexuality,* edited by Claus Overzier (Academic Press, New York and London, 1963). See also, for instance: "Development of Sexual Characteristics," by A.D. Jost in *Science Journal,* Volume 6, No. 6 (especially the chart on page 71) which indicates the variety of "sex characteristics" which occurs in normal females and males; and "Growth and Endocrinology of the Adolescent," by J. M. Tanner in *Endocrine and Genetic Diseases of Childhood,* edited by L. Gardner (Saunders, Philadelphia & London, 1969), which tries to give clinical standards for evaluating the hormonal status of adolescent youth, and in which the author characterizes individuals which are well within the normal curve for males as "feminized males," thus, by implication, as "abnormal" males; and similarly, *mutatis mutandis,* for females.

4. See, for example, *Sexual Suicide,* by George F. Gilder (Quadrangle, New York, 1979). For an eloquent example of the Victorian version of this anxiety and the world view which underlies it, see "The Emancipation of Women," by Frederic Harrison in *Fortnightly Review,* CCXCVII, October 1, 1891, as quoted in a talk given by Sandra Siegel at the Berkshire Conference on Women's History, April 1981, entitled "Historiography, 'Decadence,' and the Legend of 'Separate Spheres' in Late Victorian England," which connects Victorian conceptions of civilization and the separateness and differentness of women and men.

5. See "Oppression," in this collection.

6. See "Feminist Leaders Can't Walk On Water," by Lorraine Masterson, *Quest: A Feminist Quarterly* (Volume II, Number 4, Spring, 1976), especially pp. 35-36 where the author refers to Paulo Freire's *Pedagogy of the Oppressed* and speaks to the special case of women's belief that our subordination is inevitable because rooted in biology.

7. Cf., the early and powerful article by Naomi Weisstein, "Psychology Constructs the Female," in *Woman in Sexist Society: Studies in Power and Powerlessness,* edited by Vivian Gornick and Barbara K. Moran (Basic Books, Inc., New York, 1971). Weisstein documents clearly that neither laypersons nor psychologists are the least bit dependable as observers of sex-correlated traits of people, and that theories of sex-difference based on "clinical experience" and based on primate studies are scientifically worthless.

THE PROBLEM THAT HAS NO NAME*

The phenomenon I analyze here is something I first began attending to under the rubric "male chauvinism." That term seems to have gone out of fashion in the circles I move in, but the phenomenon hasn't. Other words for it are 'sexism', 'male supremicism', 'misogyny'. But none of them quite seem to fit; and notice that like 'male chauvinism' they are recently coined terms, made up by women trying to find a name for something their native language has no name for. It wants an "ism" sort of word, for it is not a single belief or simple attitude, but an attitudinal-conceptual-cognitive-orientational complex. Looking at it is looking at a cross section of a world view. One feels that with time and patience enough, one could reconstruct the entire multidimensional world view from what one can see in this slice. I made up the words 'phallism' and 'phallist' for this complex and the beast it belongs to, but the novelty and strangeness of the term bothers me. It suggests that the beast is novel or strange, whereas, in fact, he is very common and familiar. I might almost want

* This is a shortened and revised version of an essay that appeared under the title "Male-Chauvinism—A Conceptual Analysis" in *Philosophy and Sex*, edited by Robert Baker and Frederick Elliston (Prometheus Books, Buffalo, New York, 1975), pp. 65-79. It appears here with the permission of the publisher.

41

to use the terms 'man-ism' and 'man' for the complex and the beast. That would actually be fine so long as I could count on people's understanding that one can't invariably tell, just by looking, who the men are, and yet that most of the folks who look like men are men, and most of those who don't aren't.

In revising this essay, I decided to stay with my made-up terms 'phallism' and 'phallist', bearing in mind that the strangeness of the terms is not an indication that the phenomenon is strange or rare but a flag notifying us that English doesn't have a word for this. Even if one has thought about this sort of thing before, it wouldn't hurt to ponder the question of why there has been no name for such a common and such a potent thing as this.

I have titled this essay, "The Problem That Has No Name," in deliberate reversal of Betty Friedan's use of that phrase as the title of the introductory chapter of *The Feminine Mystique*.[1] That book locates the problem *in women.* "The problem" as she stated it is that women are mysteriously dissatisfied with domesticity. Because she focused on women only of a certain race and class, and because she did not have a global or a radical perspective, she did not see that all women, even those who perforce have a lot more than domesticity to cope with, "want something more" and that this wanting (and also wanting a good deal *less* of some other things) is not a problem. A book about *the problem* would have to be a book about men, not about women. This essay is, in a way, a gesture toward that book.*

Summary, 1982

---

* I am heavily indebted to Carolyn Shafer, with whom I thoroughly and profitably discussed all parts of this essay at all stages of its development; her contribution is substantial. I also profited from discussion with an audience of philosophers and others at Michigan State University, and an audience at a meeting of the Eastern Division of the Society of Women in Philosophy, in April 1974, at Wellesley College.

I

Feminists have always been sensitive to the conflation of the concepts of *Man* and *male*. People tend (and are explicitly taught) to think of distinctively human characteristics as distinctively masculine, e.g. rationality, and to credit distinctively human products or achievements like culture, technology, language and science to men, that is, to males. Blended with this there is a (distinctively human?) tendency to romanticize and aggrandize the human species and to derive from one's rosy picture of it a sense one's individual specialness and superiority.

Identifying with the human race, with the species, seems to involve a certain consciousness of the traits or properties one has just as a human being. In this, one generally focuses on those distinguishing traits which one can easily construe as marking the elevation of this species above the rest of the animal kingdom—such traits as speech, reason and moral sensibility. Being the highest animals, the crowning achievement of evolution, we feel it morally acceptable, even laudable, to treat members of other species with contempt, condescension and patronage. We supervise their safety, we decide what is best for them, we cultivate and train them to serve our needs and please us, we arrange that they shall be fed and sheltered as we please and shall breed and have offspring at our convenience. And often our concern for their welfare is sincere and our affection genuine.

Every single human being, simply as a human being and regardless of personal virtue, ability or accomplishment is presumed by virtually all of us to have these rights and in some cases duties with respect to members of any other species. All human beings can, we assume, be absolutely confident of their unquestionable superiority over every creature of every other species, however clever, willful, intelligent or independently capable of survival that creature may be. This set of presumptions might suitably be called *humanism*.

Phallism is a form of humanism. It is an assumption of
superiority, with accompanying rights and duties, that is seen
as not requiring justification by personal virtue or individual
merit and is taken to justify a contemptuous or patronizing
attitude toward certain others. The phallist, confusing *Man*
and *man*, meets women with humanist contempt and patronage.

It will be noted that women are not the only human creatures that are not, or not generally, treated with the respect
apparently due members of so elevated a species as ours. This
is quite true. An arrogation of rights and duties fully analo-
gous to humanism is carried out also in relation to infants, the
aged, the ill, those labeled insane or criminal, and by members
of dominant races in relation to members of subordinated
races. It turns out that in the eyes of any particular human
creature, only certain of the other beings that are human (*versus* canine, etc.) are taken to be participants in species superiority; others are taken to be something less because they are
"defective" or "underdeveloped" or members of some other
non-fully-human species. The point here is that phallists place
female humans (of any race, age, fitness or moral character)
in just this latter category. The words 'defective' and 'underdeveloped' are actually used with deadly seriousness in descriptions of female psychology and anatomy broadcast by
some of those assumed to have professional competence in
such things. And some men say, and sometimes write, that
women are of another species than their own.

Given this degree of acquaintance with the phallist, one can
see why women complain of not being treated as persons by
these people. Those human creatures that we approach and
treat with not the slightest trace of humanistic contempt are
those we recognize unqualifiedly as persons. The phallist approaches females with a superiority and condescension that
almost all of us take (often wrongly) to be more or less appropriate to encounters with members of other species and
with "defective" or not fully developed members of our own.
This just means that phallists do not treat women as persons.

II

The phallist does not treat women as persons. The obvious question is: Does he withhold this treatment in full awareness that women are persons? Are we dealing with simple malice? Given the benefits and privileges accorded to those treated as persons, there is every reason to think selfishness and greed would generate a great deal of such intelligent wickedness.* But given their remarkable lack of self-consciousness or guilt, it seems that some phallists must be involved in something more complex and less forthright than that. The phallist can arrange things so that he does not experience females as persons in the first place and thus will not have to justify to himself his failure to treat them as persons.

Experience with cases, such as with people who are extremely ill in certain ways, reveals that, in practice, one generally applies the notion of a person according to the presence of certain behavior in certain circumstances. The appearance of this behavior in these circumstances is presumed to indicate the presence of, and certain levels of, abilities and concerns that one thinks of as characteistic or definitive of persons. When one does not believe the being in question has those abilities or concerns in suitable amounts or levels, one's orientation to it changes, in some cases moving toward an attitude of caretaking; in others, perhaps, toward abandonment.

Given this general picture, one can easily see that the possibilities for failing to attribute personhood to persons are plentiful. (1) One can observe a creature that is in fact "person-behaving" and come away simply not believing or not know-

---

* I take the phrase 'intelligent wickedness' from the title given a speech by William Lloyd Garrison which is included in *Feminism: The Essential Historical Writings,* edited by Miriam Schneir (Vintage Books, New York, 1972). In it he points out that men "manifest their guilt to a demonstration, in the manner in which they receive this movement [feminism] . . .they who are only ignorant, will never rage, and rave, and threaten, and foam, when the light comes. . . ." One cannot but believe that there are also some who, well aware of the point Garrison makes, prudently refrain from foaming in public.

ing that the behavior took place; for example, a waitress may anticipate one's readiness for coffee and bring the coffee, all in full view, and one may not know that a very person-ish performance has just gone on here. (2) One can observe certain behavior and take it as a manifestation of a lower degree or smaller range of abilities and concerns than it in fact manifests; the performances of secretaries, for instance, are often subject to this sort of misjudgment. (3) One may observe circumstances that are adverse to the manifestation of the relevant abilities, judge these circumstances to have been optimal, and conclude from the nonappearance of the abilities in these "optimal" circumstances that they are not present; Black children in white schools (and women of any race in university classrooms) are routinely subjected to this sort of treatment. I have no doubt that people who avoid perceiving women as persons do all of these sorts of things, singly and in combination. But another more vicious device is at hand. It is not a matter of simple misrepresentation of presented data, but a matter of rigging the data and then taking it at face value.

The characteristic abilities and cares of persons are manifest only in certain suitable circumstances. One can ensure that an individual will seem not to have these abilities by arranging for the false appearance that the individual has been in suitable circumstances for their manifestation. The individual will not in fact have been in suitable circumstances, which guarantees that the abilities will not be manifest; but it will seem that the individual was in suitable circumstances and the observer will reasonably take it that the individual lacks the abilities in question. Then to wrap it up, one can overlook the fact that one manipulated the data, take the position of the naive observer, and conclude for oneself that the individual lacks the abilities. Parents are often in a position to do this sort of trick. Presenting their daughters with unsuitable learning situations which they will take to be suitable, they convince themselves that they have discovered the children's inability to learn those things. A simple example is that of a father's attempt to teach his daughter to throw a baseball. He goes through a few superficial and short-lived efforts and shortly declares failure—her failure—without having engaged anything like the perseverence and ingenuity that he would have engaged in the training of his son. It doesn't take very many such exercises to establish the father's conviction that the daughter is incapable of the physical competence necessary to be able to defend one's physical integrity, and therefore that she is incapable of the kind of independence and autonomy he associates with full or mature personhood.

But even this does not exhaust the maneuvers available to the phallist. A critical central range of the traits and abilities that go into a creature's being a person are traits and abilities that can be manifest only in circumstances of interpersonal interaction wherein another person maintains a certain level of communicativeness and cooperativeness. One cannot, for instance, manifest certain kinds of intelligence in interactions with persons who have a prior conviction of one's stupidity; one's clever pun is heard as a clumsy misuse of a word or as a *non sequitor.* One cannot manifest sensitivity or discretion in interactions with someone who is distrustful and will not share relevant information. It is this sort of thing that opens up the possibility for the most elegant of the phallist's strategies, one that very nicely combines simplicity and effectiveness. He can avoid seeing the critical central range of a woman's abilities and concerns simply by being uncooperative and uncommunicative and can, at the same time, be so without knowing he has been. The ease with which one can be uncooperative and uncommunicative while believing oneself to be the opposite is apparent from the most casual acquaintance with common interpersonal problems. The manipulation of the circumstances is easy, the falsification is easy, and the effects are broad and conclusive.

The power and rigidity of the phallist's refusal to experience women as persons is exposed in a curious perceptual flip he performs when he is forced or tricked into experiencing a particular being as a person who is in fact female. Those of her traits that he thinks of as distinctively female, which in another situation would irresistably draw his attention, now may go virtually unnoticed, and she becomes "one of the boys." Confronted with the dissonant appearance of a female person in a situation where he is unable to block out the fact that she is a person, he blocks out the fact that she is female.

The frustration of trying to function as a person in interaction with someone who is exercising this kind of control over others and over his own perceptions, and is not acknowledging it, is one of the primary sources of feminist rage.

III

It has been assumed in the preceding section that it is obvious that women are persons. Otherwise, failure to perceive women as persons would not have to involve all this fooling around. Some women, however, clearly think there is some point in asserting that they are persons, and some women's experience is such that they are inclined to say that they are denied personhood.

To some, there seems to be certain silliness about the assertion that women are persons, which derives from the fact that almost everybody, female and male alike, seems to *agree* that women are people. But in many instances this constitutes no more than an acceptance of the fact that females are biologically human (not canine, etc.) and have certain linguistic capacities and emotional needs. In accepting this, one is committed to no more than the belief that women should be treated humanely, as we are enjoined to treat the very ill, the elderly and members of whatever race(s) we take to be below our own in the pecking order. But the personhood of which I am speaking here is "full" personhood. I am speaking of unqualified participation in the radical "superiority" of the species, without justification by individual virtue or achievement—unqualified membership of that group of beings that may approach all other creatures with humanist arrogance. Members of this group are to be treated not humanely but with respect. It is plain that not everybody, not even almost everybody, agrees that women belong to this group. Asserting that they do is hardly saying something so generally obvious as to be unworthy of assertion.

The other claim—that women are denied personhood—can also seem strange, but there is something to it. To some, the concept of a person seems somewhat like the concepts that are sometimes called "institutional," such as the concepts of a lawyer or a knight. To some it seems that 'person' denotes a social or institutional role and that one may be allowed or forbidden to adopt that role. It seems that we (persons) have some sort of power to admit creatures to personhood. I do not find this view plausible, but it surely recommends itself to some, and it must be attractive to the phallist, who would fancy the power to create persons. His refusal to perceive women as persons could then be taken by him as an exercise of this power. Some phallists give every sign of accepting this or a similar view, and some women seem to be taken in by it too. Hence, some women are worked into the position of asking to be granted personhood. It is a peculiar position for a person to be in, but such are the almost inevitable effects of phallist manipulation on those not forewarned. Of course, one cannot make what is a person not a person by wishing it so. And yet some vague impression lingers that phallists do just that—and it is not without encouragement that it lingers.

Even apart from the cases of institutional concepts, there is in the employment of concepts, as in the employment of words, a certain collective subjectivity. Every concept has some standard use or uses in some community—the "conceptual community" whose usage fixes its correct application. While admitting that various hedges and qualifications should be made here, one may say that, generally, if everyone in the community where the concept Y is in general use declares Xs to be Ys, then Xs are Ys. For concepts employed only by specialists or, say, used only within certain neighborhoods, the relevant conceptual communities consist of those specialists or the residents of those neighborhoods. In general, the conceptual community whose use of a concept fixes its correct application simply consists of all the people who use it. To determine its correct application, one identifies the people who use it and then describes or characterizes their use of it.

The concept of a person is a special case here. To discover the range of application of the concept of a person, one might identify the conceptual community in which that concept is used. It consists, of course, of all the persons who use the concept. To identify that conceptual community, one must decide which creatures are persons. The upshot is that the phallist who self-deceptively adjusts the range of application of the concept of a person is also manipulating appearances with respect to the constitution of the conceptual community. Males who live their lives under the impression that only males are persons (and in the belief that this impression is shared by others) will see *themselves* (the persons) as completely constituting the conceptual community and thence take *their* agreement in the (overt) application of the concept of a person as fixing its correct application, much as we all take our agreement in the application of the concept of a tree as fixing its correct application. We do not have the power to make what is a tree not a tree, but the collective subjectivity of conceptual correctness can be mistaken to mean that we do. Nor could the phallists, if they did constitute the conceptual community, thereby have the power to make what is a person not a person. But it is here, I think, that one finds the deepest source of the impression that women are *denied* personhood.

The self-deceptive denial that women are (full) persons adds up to an attempt to usurp the community's control over concepts in general by denying females membership in the conceptual community, or rather, by failing to see that they are members of the conceptual community. The effect is not simply the exclusion of females from the rights and duties of full persons but is a conceptual banishment that ensures that their objections to this exclusion simply do not fit into the resulting conceptual scheme. Hence the phallist's almost incredible capacity for failure to understand what on earth feminists are talking about. His self-deception is locked into his conceptual framework, not simply as his analytic or *a priori* principles are, but in the underlying determinants of its entire structure and content. The self-deception fixes his conception of the constitution of the conceptual community whose existence makes conceptualization possible and whose collective perceptions determine in outline its progress. The rejection of females by phallists is both morally and conceptually profound. The refusal to perceive females as persons is conceptually profound because it excludes females from that community whose conceptions of things one allows to influence one's own concepts—it serves as a police lock on a closed mind. Furthermore, the refusal to treat women with the respect due to persons is in itself a violation of a moral principle that seems to many to be *the* founding principle of all morality. This violation of moral principle is sustained by an active manipulation of circumstances that is systematic and habitual and unacknowledged. The exclusion of women from the conceptual community simultaneously excludes them from the moral community. So the manipulation here is designed not just to dodge particular applications of moral principles but to narrow the moral community itself, and is therefore particularly insidious. It is the sort of thing that leavens the moral schizophrenia of the gentle, honest, god-fearing racist monster, the self-anointed *übermensch,* and other moral deviates. The phallist is confined with the worst of moral company in a self-designed conceptual closet—and he has taken great pains to ensure that this escape will not be abetted by any woman.

NOTES

1. Dell Publishing Company, New York, 1963.

IN AND OUT OF HARM'S WAY: ARROGANCE AND LOVE*

INTRODUCTION

Most of this essay is devoted to constructing an account of
some of the mechanisms of the exploitation and enslavement
of women by men in phallocratic culture. Understanding
such things is obviously important in a general way to feminist theory and strategies: it is essential, as they say, to know
your enemy. But there is a more specific need of feminist
theorists and activists which these analyses also address, at
another level. This is the need to locate a point of purchase
for a radical feminist vision.

The accounts here of the mechanisms of exploitation and
enslavement yield up a vivid picture of a kind of harm char-
acteristically done the victims of these operations. Seeing
these things as *harmful* is fundamental to my belief that wom-
en's being subjected to such machinations is an evil. This is a

---

* In working out the materials in this essay, I benefited from discussion
with C. Shafer in many ways and to a degree which cannot be reflected
in particular footnotes to particular points.

place where a feminist politics can begin; but it cannot end here. When we see the effects of these machinations as harm, we implicitly invoke a contrast between the victims and the female human animal unharmed (unharmed, at least, by these particular processes). Although such an animal may be unknown in contemporary human experience, we are committed at least to an abstract conception of her. More than an abstract conception is needed if we are not simply to condemn but to resist effectively or escape. For that we need a revolutionary vision, which in turn requires that we have rich images of such an animal.

Feminist imaginings of women not harmed by men's exploitation and enslavement, like the similar imaginings of other revolutionary visionaries, have often been malnourished on sentimentality and contempt. We soar on the evidence of women's achievements and dreams of Amazon perfection and sink in the evidence of our mediocrity and the morass of our own internalized woman-hating. If it is important to imagine women untouched by phallocratic machinations, then we must take care to discover what we can know here and now on which that imagining can be fed.

The analyses in the body of this essay tell us some of what we need to know. They suggest general correctives to poor vision. They enhance our understanding of the harm done women by the processes of subordination and enslavement, and so facilitate our understanding of the creature who is harmed. The harm lies in what these processes do to women; the analyses make clearer what these processes produce, as product. Understanding something of the stages and goals of the processing, one can see what shapes and qualities it imposes. This, in turn, suggests something of the nature of the being which is processed: one can reason that this being would not have had those shapes and those qualities if left unmolested. This sort of thinking back through phallocratic process turns out to provide valuable clues for the feminist visionary.

COERCION

To coerce is to make or force someone to do something. This seems pretty straightforward, but some of the uses of this concept are not, and one might get confused. The law in some states and general opinion in most places would have it, for instance, that an act is not rape unless the woman's engagement in sexual intercourse is coerced, and will not count the act as coerced unless the alleged victim of the alleged crime is literally physically overcome to the point where the rapist (or rapists) literally physically controls the movements of the victim's limbs and the location and position of her body. In any other case she is seen as choosing intercourse over other alternatives and thus as not being coerced. The curious thing about this interpretation of coercion is that it has the consequence that there is no such thing as a person being coerced into *doing* something. For if the movements of one's limbs and the location and position of one's body are not physically under one's control, one surely cannot be said to have *done* anything, except perhaps at the level of flexing one's muscles in resistance to the force. Given this way of thinking, one could reason that if one did anything (beyond the level of flexing muscles), then it would follow that one was not coerced, and in the sense of 'free' that only means *not coerced,* all actions and all choices would be free.

Sartre took this economical route to freedom and embraced the absurd conclusion as profundity:

> If I am mobilized in a war, this war is *my* war; it is
> in my image and I deserve it. I deserve it first because
> I could always get out of it by suicide or by desertion. . . .
> For lack of getting out of it, I have *chosen* it. This can
> be due to inertia, to cowardice in the face of public
> opinion, or because I prefer certain other values to the
> value of the refusal to join the war. . . . Any way you
> look at it, it is a matter of choice. . . . Therefore we
> must agree with the statement by J. Romains, "In war
> there are no innocent victims." If therefore I have pre-

ferred war to death or to dishonor, everything takes
place as if I bore the entire responsibility for this war.
. . . There was no compulsion here.[1]

It should not be surprising that the same small mind, embracing a foolish consistency, cannot recognize rape when he sees
it and employs a magical theory of "bad faith" to account for
its evidence. (In the face of the woman denying forthrightly
that she experiences pleasure in coitus with her husband, the
psychiatrist's observation that she "dreads" the experience,
and the woman's report that she deliberately averts her attention from the act and the sensations, Sartre insists that what
she dreads and tries to distract herself from is "pleasure" and
that the woman is self-deceived.)[2] The "frigid" woman does,
after all, choose intercourse over suicide; this is sufficient to
convince Sartre that she cannot be a victim and there can be
no compulsion here.

It is by this kind of reasoning that we are convinced that
women's choices to enter and remain within the institutions
of heterosexuality, marriage and motherhood are free choices,
that prostitution is a freely chosen life, and that all slaves who
have not risen up and killed their masters or committed suicide have freely chosen their lots as slaves.

But choice and action obviously can take place under coercion. The paradigm of coercion is *not* the direct and over-
powering application of force to move or arrange someone's
body and limbs. The situation of coercion must be one in
which choice and action do take place and in which the victim's body and limbs are moved under the victim's own steam,
their motions determined by the victim's own perception and
judgment. Hence, in the standard case, the force involved in
coercion is applied at some distance, and the will of the coerced agent must somehow be engaged in the determination
of the bodily movements.

The general strategy involved in all coercion is exemplified
in the simple case of armed robbery. You point a gun at
someone and demand that she hand over her money. A moment before this she had no desire to unburden herself of her

money, no interest in transferring her money from her possession to that of another; but the situation has changed, and
now, of all the options before her, handing over her money
seems relatively attractive. Under her own steam, moving her
own limbs, she removes her money from her pocket and hands
it to you. Her situation did not just change, of course. *You
changed it.*

What you did (and I think this is the heart of coercion) was
to arrange things so that of the options available, the one that
was the least unattractive or the most attractive was the very
act you wanted the victim to perform. *Given* those options,
and the victim's judgments and priorities, she chooses and
acts. Nobody else controls her limbs or makes that judgment
for her. The elements of coercion lie not in her person, mind
or body, but in the manipulation of the circumstances and
manipulation of the options.*

It will be noted by the clever would-be robber that it does
not matter in such a situation whether the gun is loaded or
not, or whether or not the robber really would or could pull
the trigger. It has only to be credible *to the victim* that the
gun is loaded and that the person holding it will fire; and
dying has to be perceived *by that victim* at that moment as
more undesireable than handing over her money. If she thinks
the person wouldn't shoot, or if she is feeling cheerfully sui-
cidal, this will not work. If it works, she has been coerced.

The structure of coercion, then, is this: to coerce someone
into doing something, one has to manipulate the situation so
that the world as perceived by the victim presents the victim
with a range of options the least unattractive of which (or the
most attractive of which) in the judgment of the victim is the

---

* What the coercer does is deliberately to create just the sort of situation Aristotle agonizes over in *Nichomachean Ethics*, III.1., wherein
"the initiative in moving the parts of the body which act as instruments
rests with the agent himself," but the agent does something which "nobody would choose to do. . .for its own sake." (*Nichomachean Ethics*,
translated by Martin Ostwald (The Library of Liberal Arts, 1962.)
Thanks to Claudia Card for reminding me of this passage.)

act one wants the victim to do. Given the centrality of the victim's perception and judgment, the plotting coercer might manipulate the physical environment but usually would proceed, at least in part, by manipulating the intended victim's perception and judgment through various kinds of influence and deception.

I assume that free and healthy humans would do much that would cohere with and contribute to the satisfaction of each other's interests and the enhancement of each other's capacities for pursuit of those interests. But for many reasons and by many causes, many people want more and different contributions and on very different terms than is consistent with the health and the will of those they want them from, however amiable, benevolent and naturally cooperative the latter may be. Hence, there is coercion. In the case of simple robbery, the coercer approaches with relatively limited goals. The structure imposed need be neither durable nor adaptable; neither the gun nor the lie need hold up to much scrutiny. But if you want another to perform for you frequently or regularly, your operation must be more complex. People don't like being coerced, and setting up a situation which is reliably and adaptably coercive requires doing something more about resistance and attempts to escape the imposed dilemma than a simple robber has to do. Hence coercion is extended, ramified and laminated as systems of oppression and exploitation.

EXPLOITATION AND OPPRESSION

Conjure for yourself an image of someone felling a tree with an ax. The ax is a tool; the tree a resource. The ax, properly used, will last for many years. The tree, properly felled, ceases to be; a log comes into being. A tool is by nature or manufacture so constituted and shaped that it is suited to a user's interest in bringing about a certain sort of effect, and so its being put to use does not require its alteration. The case is otherwise with resources or materials; their uses or exploitations typically transform them. Trees become wood which becomes pulp which becomes paper. At each stage the relations of the parts, the composition, and the condition of the thing used are significantly altered in or by the use. The parts and properties of the thing or stuff were not initially organized with reference to a certain purpose or *telos*; they are altered and rearranged so that they *are* organized with reference to that *telos*. A transforming manipulation is characteristic of this kind of using, of the exploitation of resources or materials.

Analogues of this occur in the exploitation of animate beings. In the case of nonhuman animals, their shapes, the relations of their parts, their constitutions and conditions, and the ways these change or move in the absence of human intervention generally suit them and their behavior to human interests in few and undependable ways. To make much use of such animals, one generally has to do some manipulation and alteration of them. Perhaps the simplest of these is just killing them—the direct analogue of felling the tree. To get nonhuman animals (draft animals, for instance) to work for them, human animals breed certain species to configurations, tempers and capacities to respond to training, and they train individuals of those species from a very young age to tolerate various bindings and harnesses and the bearing of various weights. These are practices which shape the developing nervous systems of the young animals, suppressing certain tendencies to twitch, shy, buck, stamp or flee. And the humans use stimulus-response conditioning to habituate the animals to certain responses to certain human actions and noises. Finally, the animals' movements are significantly shaped and restricted by harnesses, braces, shafts and various other paraphernalia that connect them to the various tools and machines their movements are to drive, push or pull. In the end, by its "second" nature, acquired through processes appropriately called "breaking" and "training" and by the physical restraints placed on it, such a beast can do very little which does *not* serve some human purpose.[3]

Some analogue of this "breaking" must be developed if a person is to exploit another person or group of persons. I have characterized oppression as a systematic network of forces and barriers which tend to the reduction, immobilization and molding of the oppressed.[4] Elsewhere I have emphasized the aspects of reduction and immobilization. Looking at oppression in its relation to exploitation brings the other aspect into sharper focus: molding, shaping. If you would harness someone else to your wagon, the other must be remodelled. Like any animal, the other is not in the nature of things ready-made to suit anyone's interests but its own. But unlike nonhuman animals, this one matches the exploiter in intelligence and fineness of physical abilities, and this one is capable of self-respect, righteousness and resentment. The human exploiter may not so easily win or outwit the human victim.

Exploitation and oppression are in tension with each other, as one would expect of things which harmonize. Efficient exploitation requires that those exploited be relatively mobile, self-animating and self-maintaining—the more so as the work in question requires greater intelligence, attention or ingenuity. But it also requires that they not be free enough, strong enough or willful enough to resist, escape or significantly misfit the situation of exploitation. While oppressive structures provide for the latter, those which consist mainly of variations on bondage and confinement are inefficient. A system which relies heavily on physical restriction both presupposes and generates resistance and attempts to escape. These in turn exacerbate the need for bondage and containment. This cycle leads to a situation in which the exploited are subjected to maximal limitation and maximal damage, including the passivity of a broken spirit.

For some exploiters, the combination of the work they want done and the milieu of power in which they operate permits them the inefficiencies wrought by the disabling and an-

nihilative effects of oppression; they may have an endless supply of humans to convert to workers, and the work may be
such as can be done by someone in shackles and/or totally
dispirited. But in many cases a relative shortage of workers,
the expense of training them, the need for employment of
workers' talents and intelligence, and sometimes (perversely
enough) the exploiter's personal attachment to the exploited,
make such inefficiency unsatisfactory. Efficient exploitation
of "human resources" requires that the structures that refer
the others' actions to the exploiter's ends must extend be-
neath the victim's skin. The exploiter has to bring about the
partial disintegration and re(mis)integration of the others'
matter, parts and properties so that as organized systems the
exploited are oriented to some degree by habits, skills, sched-
ules, values and tastes to the exploiter's ends rather than, as
they would otherwise be, to ends of their own. In particular,
the manipulations which adapt the exploited to a niche in another's economy must accomplish a great reduction of the
victim's intolerance of coercion.

The best solutions to the problem are those which dissolve
it. What the exploiter needs is that the will and intelligence
of the victim be disengaged from the projects of resistance
and escape but that they not be simply broken or destroyed.
Ideally, the dis-integration and mis-integration of the victim
should accomplish the detachment of the victim's will and
intelligence from the victim's own interests and their attachment to the interests of the exploiter. This will effect a dis-
placement or dissolution of self-respect and will undermine
the victim's intolerance of coercion. With that, the situation
transcends the initial paradigmatic form or structure of coercion; for if people don't mind doing what you want them
to do, then, in a sense, you can't really be *making* them do it.
In the limiting case, the victim's will and intelligence are
wholly transferred to a full engagement in the pursuit of the
dominating person's interests. The "problem" had been that
there were two parties with divergent interests; this sort of
solution (which is very elegant, as that word is used in logic)

is to erase the conflict by reducing the number of interested parties to one.* This radical solution can properly be called "enslavement."

ENSLAVEMENT

The mechanisms of enslavement, in cases where it is deliberately and self-consciously carried out, have been studied and documented in, among other cases, European colonization of Africa and the enslavement of Blacks and indigenous peoples in the "New World." Kathleen Barry has documented them in her book, *Female Sexual Slavery*,[5] in the case of what has been called by the misnomer "white slavery"—the enslavement of women and girls for service as prostitutes, wives, concubines and in the production of pornography. I want to draw on this latter work here because this is the category of slavery that is specific to the system of oppression which subordinates women to men.

Many feminists have found it illuminating to compare the situations of women in general to enslavement, or have seen the situations of women as forms of enslavement. For people in the United States, the use of the concept of slavery can usually be heard only as a reference to the experience and institutions of enslavement of Blacks by whites in the United States. For many reasons, such a comparison between women generally and Blacks in pre-Civil War enslavement is misleading and politically suspect.[6] But the literal enslavement of women for sexual service (frequently for both sexual and domestic service) is a venerated, vigorous, current and universal institution of male-dominated cultures which

---

* The foregoing discussion may seem to present a picture of exploiters which exaggerates their inhumanity. I recommend one read or re-read such texts as Machiavelli's *The Prince*, Orwell's *1984* and *The Report From Iron Mountain on the Possibility and Desirability of Peace* (Dell, New York, 1967), to recover a suitable sense of proportion.

routinely victimizes girls and women of all racial, economic and ethnic affiliations all over the world. It is this institution that is the appropriate object of reference when one explores the ways in which women's situations are like, or are forms of, slavery.

According to Barry, the strategy for converting a half-grown willful girl or a reasonably independent and competent woman to a servile prostitute or a passive concubine has three stages: Abduction, Seasoning and Criminalization.

Under the heading of Abduction come kidnapping and seduction, or any other act by which the abductor can remove the girl or woman from a setting which is familiar to her to a setting which is totally unfamiliar to her, where she has no allies and no knowledge of what resources are potentially available. Usually he drugs her. When she comes to consciousness of her predicament, she is temporally disoriented and ignorant of where she is (what city, what floor of the building, etc.). The victim has very little information about her surroundings, dulled wits for assimilating what information she does have, and no reliable "other" to criticize or validate her perceptions or judgments. In other words, the abductor has stripped her of the most ordinary powers and resources which even the most socially powerless people usually retain.* She is frightened and oriented to escape, but he has imposed on her by force a condition in which she can do almost nothing in her own behalf.

The next stage is Seasoning.

While he holds her in captivity and isolation, he brutalizes the victim in as many ways as there are to brutalize. Rape. Beatings. Verbal and physical degradation. Deprivation. Intense and enduring discomfort. Credible threats of murder.

The abductor's brutality functions in several ways. By placing the victim in a life-threatening and absolutely aversive situation, he maximizes the urgency of the victim's taking action in her own behalf while making it utterly impossible for

---

* Except, in many cases, those in "mental institutions" or prisons.

her to do so. This puts maximum force into the processes of alienating her from herself through total helplessness. The result is radical loss of self-esteem, self-respect and any sense of capacity or agency.* The brutality also establishes intimacy, both by being invasive and by the intensity of the one-on-one contact. At a certain point, the abductor shifts from unabating brutality to intermittent and varying brutality. This creates occasions for positive feeling on the part of the victim. She is now in a world of distorted moral proportion where not being beaten, not being under threat of imminent death, being permitted to urinate when she needs to, etc., have become occasions for gratitude. Gratitude is a positive and a binding affect. The intimacy is intensified. From now on, any time the man is not torturing her she feels herself to be relatively well treated. The process of reconstructing the elements of the person into the shape of a slave has begun.

The shift to less constant abuse is also a perverse kind of empowerment of the victim. After having been in a situation where her presence as agent has been reduced to nothing, she now has the opportunity to try to act in support of her physical survival. She can try to discover what pleases and what displeases the man, and try to please him and avoid displeasing him, thereby avoiding or postponing beatings and degradation, or being killed. She had been annihilated as an agent; when she is restored to agency, it is kept at a remove from her own interests and self-preservation. She can act indirectly and negatively in the interest of her physical survival and freedom from pain by trying to behave in ways which will forestall or avoid the man's abuse, but any direct presence of herself to herself, any directly self-preserving or self-serving behavior, will displease him and thus be counterproductive.

---

* It is interesting to note that in *Story of O,* a classic of sado-masochistic pornography, O is forbidden at this point in her "training" and ever after to touch her own genitals or breasts, which she is inclined to do to comfort herself. She is instructed that they belong to the men. (*Story of O,* by Pauline Reage [Grove Press, New York, 1965.])

If he is any good at this, the man will make it a point to be arbitrary and capricious in his pleasures and displeasures and to be very brutal when he is brutal. This will make the victim's task of anticipating his will extremely difficult and keep the stakes high. All of this draws her closer to him: her attention will be on him constantly and exclusively; her every resource of intelligence, will and sensitivity will be drawn into the most intense engagement with and focus upon him. She is likely to become "clinging" and "possessive"—not wanting to let him out of her sight. All of the will and resources she would draw upon to survive are thus channeled to the service of his interests.

The final stage, Criminalization, is necessary in order for the abductor to return the woman and his relationship with her to a more public sphere where he can turn the newly-wrought relationship to his economic benefit. He forces the woman or girl to engage in or be an accomplice to some criminal act or acts—larceny, drug traffic, murder, prostitution, kidnapping. By this she becomes and knows she becomes a criminal, part of the "underworld." Now she cannot return to family or friends, or turn to the police. As a female and a criminal she has nowhere to escape to and a great deal to be protected from. Her procurer and his associates become her protectors from the violence and scorn of the straight society. She now depends on him for protection from fates worse than he: he who is familiar, in whose domain she probably can survive by being and doing whatever he wants, and in whose world she will find the only acceptance, economic viability or social interaction and emotional life now available to her.

She is now his.

Let us review the metaphysics of this process. Brutality and radical helplessness create a fissure: the animal intelligence has no vehicle; the animal body misjudges and is inappropriately grateful. The intelligent body ceases to be: intelligence and bodilyness are sundered, unable to ground or defend each other or themselves. Mind and body, thus made separate, are then reconnected, but only indirectly: their interactions and communications now mediated by the man's will and interest. Mind and body can preserve themselves only by subordinating each other to him. The woman or girl now serves herself only by serving him, and can interpret herself only by reference to him. He has rent her in two and grafted the raw ends to himself so she can act, but only in his interest. She has been annexed and is his appendage.

In the limiting case, the slave is a robot: its behavior determined by the interests of another, its will by the will of another, its body functioning as a vehicle of another. But the condition of the slave, as I see it, is not exactly that which Mary Daly called "robotitude" and de Beauvoir called "only not dying."[7] The slave's substance is assimilated to the master— a transference Ti-Grace Atkinson called "metaphysical canni-

"By marriage, the husband and wife are one person in law; that is, the very being or legal existence of the woman is suspended during the marriage, or at least is incorporated and consolidated into that of the husband; under whose wing, protection, and cover, she performs everything." Sir William Blackstone, *Commentaries on the Laws of England,* London, 1813 (I, p. 444).

In a liberal college town in the United States in the late 70s, a woman went to get a library card at the local public library. She was told she could not get it without her husband's signature; a firm policy; no, she would need no one else's signature if she were single. This is true.

balism."[8] Although the slave is not engaged in "surpassing herself," she *is* engaged in surpassing: she is engaged in the master's "surpassing" *him*self. Her substance is organized toward his "transcendence."

THE ARROGANT EYE

The idea of there being more than one body's worth of substance, will and wit lined up behind one's projects has its appeal. As one woman said, after going through the reasons, "My God, who *wouldn't* want a wife?"[9] Ti-Grace Atkinson pointed out in her analysis of the roots of oppression that there is an enormous gap between what one can do and what one can imagine doing. Humans have what she referred to as a "constructive imagination" which, though obviously a blessing in some ways, also is a source of great frustration. For it provides a constant tease of imagined accomplishments and imagined threats—to neither of which are we physically equal.[1]
equal.[10] The majority of people do not deal with this problem and temptation by enslaving others overtly and by force (though the processes which capture the batterer's wife and attach her to him are, as Barry pointed out, very like the processes of the procurer). But many, many people, most of them male, are in a cultural and material position to accomplish, to a great degree, the same end by other means and under other descriptions, means and descriptions which obscure to them and to their victims the fact that their end is the same. The end: acquisition of the service of others. The means: variations on the same theme of dis-integrating an integrated human organism and grafting its substance to oneself.

The Bible says that all of nature (including woman) exists for man. Man is invited to subdue the earth and have domin-

ion over every living thing on it, all of which is said to exist
"to you" "for meat."[11] Woman is created to be man's helper.
This captures in myth Western Civilization's primary answer
to the philosophical question of man's place in nature: everything that is is resource for man's exploitation. With this
world view, men see with arrogant eyes which organize everything seen with reference to themselves and their own interests. The arrogating perceiver is a teleologist, a believer that
everything exists and happens for some purpose, and he tends
to animate things, imagining attitudes toward himself as the
animating motives. Everything is either "for me" or "against
me." This is the kind of vision that interprets the rock one
trips on as hostile, the bolt one cannot loosen as stubborn,
the woman who made meatloaf when he wanted spaghetti as
"bad" (though he didn't say what he wanted). The arrogant
perceiver does not countenance the possibility that the Other
is independent, indifferent. The feminist separatist can only
be a man-hater; Nature is called "Mother."

The arrogant perceiver falsifies—the Nature who makes
both green beans and *Bacillus botulinus* doesn't give a passing damn whether humans live or die[12]—but he also coerces
the objects of his perception into satisfying the conditions his
perception imposes. He tries to accomplish in a glance what
the slave masters and batterers accomplish by extended use
of physical force, and to a great extent he succeeds. He manipulates the environment, perception and judgment of her
whom he perceives so that her recognized options are limited,
and the course she chooses will be such as coheres with his
purposes. The seer himself is an element of her environment.
The structures of his perception are as solid a fact in her situation as are the structures of a chair which seats her too low
or of gestures which threaten.

How one sees another and how one expects the other to
behave are in tight interdependence, and how one expects
another to behave is a large factor in determining how the
other does behave. Naomi Weisstein, in "Psychology Con-

structs the Female," reviewed experiments which show dramatically that this is true.

> For instance, in one experiment subjects were to assign numbers to pictures of men's faces, with high numbers representing the subject's judgment that the man in the picture was a successful person, and low numbers representing the subject's judgment that the man in the picture was an unsuccessful person. One group of experimenters was told that the subjects tended to rate the faces high; another group of experimenters was told that the subjects tended to rate the faces low. Each group of experimenters was instructed to follow precisely the same procedure: they were required to read to subjects a set of instructions and to *say nothing else.* For the 375 subjects run, the results shows clearly that those subjects who performed the task with experimenters who expected high ratings gave high ratings, and those subjects who performed the task with experimenters who expected low ratings gave low ratings.[13]

When experimenters think the rats they are working with were bred for high intelligence, the rats they are working with learn faster; when the experimenters think their rats were bred for low intelligence, the rats learn less well. And children believed by their teachers to have high IQs show dramatic increases in their IQs. Weisstein concludes: "The concreteness of the changed conditions produced by expectations is a fact, a reality. . . . In some extremely important ways, people are what you expect them to be, or at least they behave as you expect them to behave."[14]

The experiments only boldly outline something we all know from experience. Women experience the coerciveness of this kind of "influence" when men perversely impose sexual meanings on our every movement. We know the palpable pressure of a man's reduction of our objection to an occasion for our instruction. Women do not so often experience ourselves imposing expectations on situations and making them stick, but some of the most awesome stories of women's successful resistance to male violence involve a woman's expecting the male assailant into the position of a little boy in the power of his mother.* The power of expectations is enormous; it should be engaged and responded to attentively and with care. The arrogant perceiver engages it with the same unconsciousness with which he engages his muscles when he writes his name.

The arrogant perceiver's expectation creates in the space about him a sort of vacuum mold into which the other is sucked and held. But the other is not sucked into his structure always, nor always without resistance. In the absence of his manipulation, the other *is* not organized primarily with reference to his interests. To the extent that she is not shaped to his will, does not fit the conformation he imposes, there is friction, anomaly or incoherence in his world. To the extent that he notices this incongruity, he can experience it in no other way than as something wrong with her. His perception is arrogating; his senses tell him that the world and everything in it (with the occasional exception of other men) is in the nature of things there *for* him, that she is by her constitution and *telos* his servant. He believes his senses. If woman does not serve man, it can only be because he is not a sufficiently skilled master or because there is something wrong with the woman. He may try to manage things better, but when that fails he can only conclude that she is defective: unnatural, flawed, broken, abnormal, damaged, sick. His norms of virtue and health are set according to the degree of congruence of the object of perception with the seer's interests. This is exactly wrong.

Though anyone might wish, for any of many reasons, to contribute to another's pursuit of her or his interests, the health and integrity of an organism is a matter of its being or-

---

* I refer here to some experience of my own, and to such stories as the Success Stories included in "Do It Yourself-Self-Defense," by Pat James, in *Fight Back: Feminist Resistance to Male Violence*, edited by Frederique Delacoste & Felice Newman (Cleis Press, 1981), p. 205.

ganized largely toward its own interests and welfare. The arrogant perceiver knows this in his own case, but he *arrogates* everything to himself and thus perceives as healthy or "right" everything that relates to him as his own substance does when he is healthy. But what's sauce for the gander is sauce for the goose. *She* is healthy and "working right" when *her* substance is organized primarily on principles which align it to *her* interests and welfare. Cooperation is essential, of course, but it will not do that I arrange everything so that you get enough exercise: for me to be healthy, *I* must get enough exercise. My being adequately exercised is logically independent of your being so.

The arrogant perceiver's perception of the other's normalcy or defectiveness is not only dead wrong, it is coercive. It manipulates the other's perception and judgment at the root by mislabeling the unwholesome as healthy, and what is wrong as right. One judges and chooses within a framework of values—notions as to what 'good' and 'good for you' pertain to. The elementary robber-coercer leaves that framework alone and manipulates only the situation. The commercial advertiser may misrepresent particular items or options as being good or good for you. But what we have in the case of the arrogant perceiver is the mis-defining of 'good' and 'healthy'. If one has the cultural and institutional power to make the misdefinition stick, one can turn the whole other person right around to oneself by this one simple trick. This is the sort of thing that makes the "reversals" Mary Daly talks about in *Gyn/Ecology* so evil and so dangerous.[15] If one does not get the concepts *right* and *wrong, healthy* and *unhealthy* right, and in particular, if one gets them wrong in the specific way determined by the arrogant eye, one *cannot* take care of oneself. This is the most fundamental kind of harm. It is, in effect, *mayhem:* a maiming which impairs a person's ability to defend herself.[16] Mayhem is very close kin both morally and logically to murder.

The procurer-enslaver, working with overt force, constructs a situation in which the victim's pursuit of her own survival

Western philosophy and science have for the most part been built on the presumption of the Intelligibility of the Universe. This is the doctrine that everything in the universe and the universe itself can, at least in principle, be understood and comprehended by human intelligence, reason and understanding.

Western philosophy and science have for the most part been committed to the Simplicity Theory of Truth: the simplest theory that accounts for the data is the true theory. (Theories are simplest which postulate the fewest entities, require the fewest hypotheses, generate predictions by the fewest calculations, etc.)

The connection seems clear: only if the truth is simple can the universe be intelligible.

But why believe either of these principles?

If someone believes that the world is made for him to have dominion over and he is made to exploit it, he must believe that he and the world are so made that he *can*, at least in principle, achieve and maintain dominion over everything. But you can't put things to use if you don't know how they work. So he must believe that he can, at least in principle, understand everything. If the world exists for man, it must be usably intelligible, which means it must be simple enough for him to understand. A usable universe is an intelligible universe is a simple universe.

If something seems to be unintelligible, you can decide it is unnatural or unreal. Or you can decide *it* is what is *really* real and then declare that you have discovered the Problem of Knowledge. Or, having declared what seems unintelligible to be the *really* real, you can claim it is, after all, intelligible, but only to the extraordinary few (who, in spite of being so few somehow can be normative of what Man really is).

. . . and so it goes with the philosophy and the science of The Arrogant Eye.

or health and her attempt to be good always require, as a matter of practical fact in that situation, actions which serve him.
In the world constructed by the arrogant eye, this same connection is established not by terror but by definition.*

The official story about men who batter women is that
they do so in large part because they suffer "low self-esteem."
What this suggests to me is that they suffer a lack of arrogance
and cannot fully believe in themselves as centers about which
all else (but some other men) revolves and to which all else
refers. Because of this they cannot effectively exercise the
power of that expectation. But as men they "know" they
are supposed to be centers of universes, so they are reduced
to trying to create by force what more successful men, men
who can carry off masculinity better, create by arrogant perception. This is, perhaps, one reason why some of the men
who do not batter have contempt for men who do.

THE LOVING EYE

The attachment of the well-broken slave to the master has
been confused with love. Under the name of Love, a willing
and unconditional servitude has been promoted as something
ecstatic, noble, fulfilling and even redemptive. All praise is

---

* Neither the arrogant perceiver nor the procurer works in a vacuum,
of course. They are supported by a culture which in many ways "soft-
ens up" their victims for them, an economy which systematically places
women in positions of economic dependence on men, and a community
of men which threatens women with rape at every turn. Also, the existence of the procurers supports the arrogant perceiver by making him
seem benign by comparison. The arrogant perceiver, in addition, has
the support of a community of arrogant perceivers, among whom are
all or most of the most powerful members of the community at large.
I do want to claim that the power of perception, even exercised without
"community support," is great; but as we normally experience it, it is
augmented enormously by its being an instance of the "normal" perceiving among those who control the material media of culture and
most other economic resources.

sung for the devoted wife who loves the husband and children she is willing to live for, and of the brave man who loves the god he is willing to kill for, the country he is willing to die for.

We can be taken in by this equation of servitude with love because we make two mistakes at once: we think, of both servitude and love, that they are selfless or unselfish. We tend to think of them as attachments in which the person is not engaged because of self-interest and does not pursue self-interest. The wife who married for money did not marry for love, we think; the mercenary soldier is despised by the loyal patriot. And the slave, we think, is selfless because she *can* do nothing but serve the interests of another. But this is wrong. Neither is the slave selfless, nor is the lover.

It is one mark of a voluntary association that the one person can survive displeasing the other, defying the other, dissociating from the other. The slave, the battered wife, the not-so-battered wife, is constantly in jeopardy. She is in a situation where she cannot, or reasonably believes she cannot, survive without the other's provision and protection, and where experience has made it credible to her that the other may kill her or abandon her if and when she displeases him. But she survives, at least for a while. She may, like Patricia Hearst, retain her own will to her own survival, in which case, what she does "for the other" is ultimately done "for herself" more consistently and more profoundly than could ever be the case in voluntary association.* In her situation of utter dependence and peril, every detail of the other's action, interests and wishes are ineluctably and directly, as a matter of empirical fact, connected to her interest in survival. She does not see the other as, or expect the other to be, organ-

---

* "Thinking it all over, I realized I would have to remain on guard at all times to avoid angering any of them. I promised myself I would never again disagree with anything any of them told me, ever. I wanted to get out alive and to see them all sent to jail for a long, long time for what they were doing to me." *Every Secret Thing*, Patricia Campbell Hearst with Alvin Moscow (Doubleday & Company, Inc., Garden City, New York, 1982), p. 57.

ized to the service of her interests (quite the contrary), but she cannot fail to interpret the other always with an eye to what will keep her from being killed or abandoned. Her eye is not arrogating, but it is the furthest thing from disinterested; she does not have the option of setting her interests aside, of not calculating them. On the other hand, the victim may survive, as *Story of O* presents her or as she is pictured in the old Geritol commercials, solely because the other wishes it. In *Story of O,* the master would be most displeased to find that O was interested in her survival for any reason other than that he wanted her to survive; that would be a last vestige of "willfulness," a telltale sign of the imperfection of her "love" for him.[17] In the Geritol commercial, the woman "takes care of herself" because her family needs her; her husband will "keep her" because she serves so devotedly. In this latter case, if it ever really is the case (as I am pessimistic enough to think it is), the slave/wife really is not motivated by self-interest, but her behavior toward and perception of the other is still not disinterested. She has assumed *his* interest. She now sees with *his* eye, his arrogant eye.

In a case like that of Patricia Hearst, in which one might say the enslavement is not perfect, the victim's self-interest is present and central—it is the fulcrum of the coercion. In the second, the victim's self-interest is simply replaced by the master's interest. In neither case is the victim disinterested or selfless in her action toward or perception of the master. She acts from her interest and for her self, or from his interest and for his self.

One who loves is not selfless either. If the loving eye is in any sense disinterested, it is not that the seer has lost herself, has no interests, or ignores or denies her interests. Any of these would seriously incapacitate her as a perceiver. What *is* the case, surely, is that unlike the slave or the master, the loving perceiver can see without the presupposition that the other poses a constant threat or that the other exists for the seer's service; nor does she see with the other's eye instead of her own. Her interest does not blend the seer and the seen, either empirically by terror or *a priori* by conceptual links forged by the arrogant eye. One who sees with a loving eye is separate from the other whom she sees. There are boundaries between them; she and the other are two; their interests are not identical; they are not blended in vital parasitic or symbiotic relations, nor does she believe they are or try to pretend they are.

The loving eye is a contrary of the arrogant eye.

The loving eye knows the independence of the other. It is the eye of a seer who knows that nature is indifferent. It is the eye of one who knows that to know the seen, one must consult something other than one's own will and interests and fears and imagination. One must look at the thing. One must look and listen and check and question.

The loving eye is one that pays a certain sort of attention. This attention can require a discipline but *not* a self-denial. The discipline is one of self-knowledge, knowledge of the scope and boundary of the self. What is required is that one know what are one's interests, desires and loathings, one's projects, hungers, fears and wishes, and that one know what is and what is not determined by these. In particular, it is a matter of being able to tell one's own interests from those of others and of knowing where one's self leaves off and another begins. Perhaps in another world this would be easy and not a matter of discipline, but here we are brought up among metaphysical cannibals and their robots. Some of us are taught we can have everything, some are taught we can have nothing. Either way we will acquire a great wanting. The wanting doesn't care about truth: it simplifies, where the truth is complex; it invents, when it should be investigating; it expects, when it should be waiting to find out; it would turn everything to its satisfaction; and what it finally thinks it cannot thus maneuver it hates. But the necessary discipline is not a denial of the wanting. On the contrary, it is a discipline of knowing and owning the wanting: identifying it, claiming it, knowing its scope, and through all this, knowing its distance from the truth.

The loving eye does not make the object of perception into something edible, does not try to assimilate it, does not reduce it to the size of the seer's desire, fear and imagination, and hence does not have to simplify. It knows the complexity of the other as something which will forever present new things to be known. The science of the loving eye would favor The Complexity Theory of Truth and presuppose The Endless Interestingness of the Universe.

The loving eye seems generous to its object, though it means neither to give nor to take, for not-being-invaded, not-being-coerced, not-being-annexed must be felt in a world such as ours as a great gift.

THE BELOVED

We who would love women, and well, who would change ourselves and change the world so that it is possible to love women well, we need to imagine the possibilities for what women might be if we lived lives free of the material and perceptual forces which subordinate women to men. The point is not to imagine a female human animal unaffected by the other humans around it, uninfluenced by its own and others' perceptions of others' interests, unaffected by culture. The point is only to imagine women not enslaved, to imagine these intelligent, willful and female bodies not subordinated in service to males, individually or via institutions (or to anybody, in any way); not pressed into a shape that suits an arrogant eye.

The forces which we want to imagine ourselves free of are a guide to what we might be when free of them. They mark the shape they mold us to, but they also suggest by implication the shapes we might have been without that molding. One can guess something of the magnitude and direction of the tendencies the thing would exhibit when free by attend-

ing to the magnitudes and directions of the forces required
to confine and shape it. For instance, much pressure is applied at the point of our verbal behavior, enforcing silence or
limiting our speech.[18] One can reason that without that force
we might show ourselves to be loquacious and perhaps prone
to oratory, not to mention prone to saying things unpleasant
to male ears. The threat of rape is a force of great magnitude
which is, among other things, applied against our movement
about the cities, towns and countryside. The implication is
that without it a great many women might prove to be very
prone to nomadic lives of exploration and adventure—why
else should so much force be required to keep us at home?

But to speak most generally: the forces of men's material
and perceptual violence mold Woman to dependence upon
Man, in every meaning of 'dependence': contingent upon;
conditional upon; necessitated by; defined in terms of; in-
complete or unreal without; requiring the support or assistance of; being a subordinate part of; being an appurtenance
to.

Dependence is forced upon us. It is not rash to speculate
that without this force, much, most or all of what most or all
of us are and do would not be contingent upon, conditional
upon, necessitated by, or subordinate to any man or what belongs to or pertains to a man, men or masculinity. What we
are and how we are, or what we would be and how we would
be if not molded by the arrogating eye, is: *not molded to
man, not dependent.*

I do not speak here of a specious absolute independence
that would mean never responding to another's need and
never needing another's response. I conceive here simply of
a being whose needs and responses are not *bound* by concepts
or by terror in a dependence upon those of another. The loving eye makes the correct assumption: the object of the seeing is *another* being whose existence and character are logically independent of the seer and who may be practically or empirically independent in any particular respect at any particular time.

It is not an easy thing to grasp the meaning or the truth of this "independence," nor is a clear or secure belief in it at all common, even among those who identify themselves as feminists. The inability to think it is one of the things that locks men in eternal infantilism; it is one of the things that makes women endlessly susceptible to deep uncertainty in our political and epistemological claims, and to nearly fatal indecisiveness in our actions.

When we try to think ourselves independent, to think ourselves women not mediated by men or Man, what we attempt is both prodigious and terrifying, since by our own wills we would be led to that fringe of the world where language and meaning let go their hold on our lives. So, understandably, we suffer failures of imagination and failures of courage.

We have to a great extent learned the arrogant boychild's vocabulary, and to identify with him and see with his eye; we have learned to think of agency and power very much as he does. What we may do when we try to imagine ourselves independent is just slip ourselves slyly into his shoes and imagine *ourselves* the center of the universe, the darlings of Mother Nature and the cherished sisters of all other women.

Much of the radical feminist art and theory which has nurtured my imagination has been characterized by occasional streaks of this kind of romanticism. Some of it is much influenced by such ideas of a "built in" perfect harmony among women and between women and Nature. Something of this sort is part of the romantic element in Mary Daly's *Gyn/Ecology;* it is in Susan Griffin's *Woman and Nature;* it is very prevalent (I do not say universal) in the literature and art of women's spirituality.[19] *The Wanderground,* a fantasy novel which has been very successful in feminist circles, develops such a romanticism quite explicitly.[20] This tendency of thought is markedly absent from two other feminist fantasy novels, *Walk To The End Of The World* and *Motherlines,*[21] and these have been, for that very reason, disliked and criticized by some feminists for not presenting a feminist vision. The same failure of imagination which has seduced some radical feminist thinking into a rose-colored vision of ourselves and Nature has much more fundamentally shaped the "civil rights" wing of feminist thought. The woman who wants "equality" in many cases simply wants to be in there *too,* as one of the men for whom men's God made everything "for meat."

It has been suggested to me that we fail in these efforts of imagination partly because we insist on reinventing the wheel. We might give womankind some credit: we might suppose that not all women lead and have lead male-mediated lives, and that the lives of the more independent women could provide material for the stimulation and correction of our imaginations. Women of exceptional gifts and creative achievements there are, and women whose lives do not follow the beaten path. But also, when one looks closely at the lives of the women presented by history or in one's own experience as exceptional, one often sees both some not-so-exceptional causal factors like the patronage of exceptional men (for which one must assume the women pay in some coin or other), and signs of peculiar fears and strange lapses of imagination.

Why did so powerful and individual a woman as Gertrude Stein speak only in code and hardly at all in public of her passionate relationship with Alice B. Toklas? Why did brilliant suffragists, white women, fail politically under the pressure of racism? Why did Simone Weil hate Jews, and why did she think suffering would make her good? Why did Simone de Beauvoir adhere to the misogynist Jean Paul Sartre? I know gifted lesbian feminist scholars who identify themselves as lesbian separatists and are passionately committed to making "the boys" in their fields recognize their work, talent and intelligence; this makes no sense. And I have heard women whose accomplishments and spirit show them capable of material and intellectual independence talking about their husbands in ways that make it inexplicable that they remain married to these men. Feminist writing, especially autobiographical writing, is full of examples of the most disappointing of all the exceptional women to whom we would turn, to whom we have turned—the mothers, grandmothers, aunts, sisters and cousins who have in our own real lives been our examples of strength, power, independence and solidarity with other women, and of whom we say, almost grieving, "She really was/is a feminist/dyke, though she would rather die than be called by that name."

The answers to the puzzles all these women present are of course very complex and individual. But I think there is at least one common thread: there is in the fabric of our lives, not always visible but always affecting its texture and strength, a mortal dread of being outside the field of vision of the arrogant eye. That eye gives all things meaning by connecting all things to each other by way of their references to one point— Man. We fear that if we are not in that web of meaning there will be no meaning: our work will be meaningless, our lives of no value, our accomplishments empty, our identities illusory. The reason for this dread, I suggest, is that for most of us , including the exceptional, a woman existing outside the field of vision of man's arrogant eye is really inconceivable.

This is a terrible disability. If we have no intuition of ourselves as independent, unmediated beings in the world, then we cannot conceive ourselves surviving our liberation; for what our liberation will do is dissolve the structures and dismantle the mechanisms by which Woman is mediated by Man. If we cannot imagine ourselves surviving this, we certainly will not make it happen.

There probably is really no distinction, in the end, between imagination and courage. We can't imagine what we can't face, and we can't face what we can't imagine. To break out of the structures of the arrogant eye we have to dare to rely on ourselves to make meaning and we have to imagine ourselves beings capable of that: capable of weaving the web of meaning which will hold us in some kind of intelligibility. We do manage this, to some extent; but we also wobble and threaten to fall, like a beginner on a bicycle who does not get up enough momentum, partly for lack of nerve.

We have correctly intuited that the making of meaning is social and requires a certain community of perception. We also are individually timid and want "support." So it is only against a background of an imagined community of ultimate harmony and perfect agreement that we dare to think it possible to make meaning. This brings us into an arrogance of our own, for we make it a prerequisite for our construction of meaning that other women be what we need them to be to constitute the harmonious community of agreement we require. Some women refuse to participate at all in this meaning construction "because feminists are divided and can't agree among themselves." Some who do participate threaten to return to the father's fold or to write others out of the movement if unanimity cannot be achieved. In other words, we threaten to fail in imagination and courage like all the other exceptional and ordinary women, if our sisters do not or will not harmonize and agree with us.

Meaning is indeed something that arises among two or more individuals and requires some degree of agreement in perception and values. (It also tends to generate the required community and the necessary degree of agreement.) The community required for meaning, however, is precisely *not* a homogenous herd, for without difference there is no meaning. Meaning is a system of connections and distinctions among different and distinguishable things. The hypothetical homogeneous community which we imagine we need *could* not be the community in which we can make ourselves intelligible, im-mediately, to and for ourselves.

The liberated woman cannot be presumed to "suit" us, and such presumption will simply keep us from actually imagining her *free;* for in our own effort of imagination, we impose upon her. If we feed our vision on images filtered through what we suppose to be our own necessities, we will be disappointed and resentful and will end up doing violence.

We need to know women as independent: subjectively in our own beings, and in our appreciations of others. If we are to know it in ourselves, I think we may have to be under the

gaze of a loving eye, the eye which presupposes our independence. The loving eye does not prohibit a woman's experiencing the world directly, does not force her to experience it by
way of the interested interpretations of the seer in whose visual field she moves. In this situation, she *can* experience directly in her bones the contingent character of her relations
to all others and to Nature. If we are to know women's independence in the being of others, I think we may have to cast
a loving eye toward them. . .and wait, and see.

NOTES

1. *Being and Nothingness,* translated by Hazel E. Barnes (Philosophical
Library, New York, 1956), p. 553.

2. Ibid., p. 54.

3. I am indebted to Carolyn Shafer both for information about the
breeding and training of domestic animals and for political interpretation of it. Se also, *Woman And Nature: The Roaring Inside Her,* by
Susan Griffin (Harper and Row, New York, 1978).

4. See the first and second essays in this collection.

5. Prentice-Hall, Englewood Cliffs, New Jersey, 1979.

6. Cf., *Ain't I A Woman: Black Women and Feminism,* by Bell Hooks
(South End Press, Boston, 1981), p. 143 and all of Chapter IV, "Racism
and Feminism."

7. *Gyn/Ecology: The Metaethics of Radical Feminism,* by Mary Daly
(Beacon Press, Boston, 1978), p. 55, and Daly's reference there to de
Beauvoir's *The Ethics of Ambiguity.*

8. *Amazon Odyssey,* by Ti-Grace Atkinson (Links Books, New York,
1974), "Metaphysical Cannibalism," pp. 56 ff.

9. "Why I Want A Wife," by Judy Syfers, *Radical Feminism,* edited by
Anne Koedt, Ellen Levine and Anita Rapone (Quadrangle, New York,
1973), pp. 60-62.

10. Atkinson, op. cit.

11. Genesis 1:29.

12. Due to Catherine Madsen, from her review of *Wanderground*, by Sally Gearhart (Persephone Press, Watertown, Massachusetts, 1979), in *Conditions No. 7*, p. 138.

13. "Psychology Constructs the Female," by Naomi Weisstein, in *Woman In Sexist Society*, edited by Vivian Gornick and Barbara K. Moran (Basic Books, Inc., New York, 1971), pp. 138-139.

14. Ibid.

15. Daly, op. cit., pp. 2, 30 and elsewhere throughout the book.

16. *Webster's Third New International Dictionary* and *The Shorter Oxford English Dictionary*.

17. *Story of O*, by Pauline Reage (Grove Press, New York, 1965). See also *Woman Hating*, by Andrea Dworkin (E.P. Dutton, New York, 1974), Chapter 3, "Woman as Victim: *Story of O*."

18. Cf., *Man-Made Language*, by Dale Spender (Routledge & Kegan Paul, London, 1980), pp. 43-50.

19. Cf., the magazine *Womanspirit*.

20. Sally Gearhart (Persephone Press, Watertown, Massachusetts, 1979).

21. *Walk To The End Of The World*, by Suzy McKee Charnas (Berkley Publishing Company, New York, 1974) and *Motherlines*, by Suzy McKee Charnas (Berkley Publishing Company, New York, 1979).

A NOTE ON ANGER*

It is a tiresome truth of women's experience that our anger is generally not well-received. Men (and sometimes women) ignore it, see it as our being "upset" or "hysterical," or see it as craziness. Attention is turned not to what we are angry about but to the project of calming us down and to the topic of our "mental stability." It is as common as dirty socks. Every woman knows it, has lived it. Men receive women's anger as incongruous and irrational and in many cases they are simply unable to improvise any way to cope with it: they strike out physically, slapping or beating the angry woman, or they retreat, covering their incompetence with something like "I can't deal with you when you're like this."[1]

I don't read men's misreading of women's anger and their inability to respond appropriately to it as wholly or always willful and malicious, as always simply a pretense put up just to frustrate the anger and avoid acting on the matter the anger is about. It has often not felt to me like simple perversity in the situations I have experienced, and this judgment is supported also by my experience on the other side of oppres-

---

* I am indebted to C.S. for valuable criticism of earlier drafts of this essay.

sion's barriers, as a white woman encountering the anger of women of color. The anger is in fact sane and sound, but its *seeming* crazy and bizarre to the receiver is also real. In many situations men really do experience women's anger as some sort of unnatural and baffling event that has no intelligible place in the causal order unless the man can see the woman as "out of order."

Though it is correct to deplore and denounce this odd combination of ignorance and incompetence as sexist (or racist), that is neither intellectually nor politically sufficient. We can, if we will, learn something from this phenomenon.

Anger seems to be a reaction to being thwarted, frustrated or harmed. It comes when your momentum is dispersed or deflected. You are going along living your life, tending your business, pursuing your project, and then you are stopped; a bureaucratic tangle, someone's unwillingness to lend reason- able assistance, the breakdown of a car. The energy that was moving you along your course cannot flow; it is blocked, it becomes turbulent. In some cases you feel frustrated, irritated, disoriented or depressed; in some cases you become angry.

The frustrating situations which generate anger, as opposed to those which merely make you displeased or depressed, are those in which you see yourself not simply as obstructed or hindered, but as wronged. You become angry when you see the obstruction or hindrance as unjust or unfair, or when you see it as due to someone's malice or inexcusable incompetence. Most of us, if we are kept from going to the concert or the ball game by the weather, are disappointed, maybe grouchy, perhaps depressed; but if we are kept from going because our partner lost the tickets, we are more likely to be angry. If a person does shake a fist at the sky in anger about the weather, she is either ridiculous or she is pretending or even believing that there is some sort of agent up there whose responsibility in this matter makes the snowstorm a wrong rather than a misfortune. Anger implies not only that the inhibition or obstruction was distressing, but that it was an offense.

To be or be perceived as wronged, you have to be or be perceived as right. Anger is always righteous. To be angry you have to have some sense of the rightness or propriety of your position and your interest in whatever has been hindered, interfered with or harmed, and anger implies a claim to such rightness or propriety. When you are not "right" or "in the right," anger is inappropriate, or impossible.* Suppose that in the midst of cooking something you realize you need mushrooms. You've seen an ad in the paper that says a particular store has a special on mushrooms. You dash off to that store but find that they don't have any mushrooms, at any price. You may be angry. But if it turns out that you misremembered the ad, and it was actually another store's ad, that will take the wind out of your sails. If you are not right in your expectation, you are not wronged in its disappointment.

There are many kinds and senses of presence, propriety, position and place, many kinds of "being in the right." I do not mean here to speak just of "rights" in some strict political or legal sense. I mean to speak of something which is the logical mate of respect.[2]

When a person is harmlessly about her business, pursuing her interests as she sees fit, employing means and using resources which are properly hers to employ, respect dictates

---

* Some people are surely careless and irresponsible in their anger and don't pay much attention to whether they are right or not, not caring much about whether their anger is appropriate or not. But I suspect that such people think they are right to get their way whether or not they are the right person, in the right circumstance, with the right expectations, etc.

that you permit her actions, and the objects and conditions
these require, to be under her control or to happen as felici-
tously as the fates will allow. If she is engaged in building
bookshelves, respect dictates that you not saunter up and
take the hammer without bothering to ask her if she's fin-
ished with it (unless, of course, you need it to defend both
your lives by braining a dangerous intruder). Whether or not
the hammer is, in a legal sense, her property, it is in her domain and associated with her by the web of connections her
purposive behavior weaves. If you walk off with it (in the
absence of some overriding factor like the intruder), your
act implies that you do not acknowledge that it is "rightful"
that the hammer be in her domain: for instance, that you
think she does not have a right to use it because she stole it;
or she ought not be making bookshelves on company time;
or she's botched it up so badly she shouldn't bother continuing anyway; or you simply don't think she or her project is
worth minimal recognition and consideration. If you think
any of these things, then there is something about her and/or
her project which you are not respecting.

The domain one acknowledges in respecting a person, a
project or act is not simply physical, encompassing physical
objects. Acknowledgement of right may dictate refraining
from making conversation which would distract a person, or
it might dictate encouraging her or not discouraging her. Her
attention, her confidence, her sense of well-being, her freedom to speak her mind, her access to knowledge and skills,
are all matters within her domain.

Anger implies a claim to domain—a claim that one is a
being whose purposes and activities require and create a web
of objects, spaces, attitudes and interests that is worthy of
respect, and that the topic of this anger is a matter rightly
within that web. You walk off with my hammer and I angrily demand that you bring it back. Implicitly, I claim that my
project is worthy, that I am within my rights to be doing it,
that the web of connections it weaves rightly encompasses
that hammer. Or you wantonly criticize my work, without

invitation, and I angrily tell you to mind your own business. Implicitly, I claim the right to do this work, the propriety of relying only on my own judgment if I wish, and the sanctity of whatever confidence I have in my abilities and the success of the project. There is something I demand that you respect.*

Being angry is usefully understood on analogy with acts the philosopher J.L. Austin called "speech acts."[3] When you say something like "I promise" or "I apologize," you do not just assert or report something about yourself, you also re-orient yourself and another person to each other. You become committed, another comes to count on you; you undo a debt, an imbalance of good and ill will is repaired. This alteration of relations requires and involves a certain cooperation from the second party. You can say, "I promise I'll write you," but also the other must take herself to be someone to whom you are obligated and must count on your doing what you said you'd do. If the second party's "uptake" is not forthcoming, the relation between the two does not take the intended shape, and the "promise" collapses. Your speech just hangs there—embarrassed, unconsummated.

Being angry at someone is somewhat like a speech act in that it has a certain conventional force whereby it sets people up in a certain sort of orientation to each other; and like a speech act, it cannot "come off" if it does not get uptake.

One woman told of this experience: She had gone to some trouble to adjust the carburetor on her car and shortly thereafter an attendant at a gas station started monkeying with it.

---

* I use examples of one person angry at one other person about one thing because they are simple paradigms. Of course one can get angry at oneself, or at many others, and a group can be angry. The picture presented here can be extended to these sorts of cases, but it is not my purpose to do that in this sketch.

She was dismayed and sharply told him to stop.* He became
very agitated and yelled at her, calling her a crazy bitch.

Other responses might have been forthcoming from the
attendant. He might have demanded to know why he should-
n't touch it; he might have defensively claimed he was only
looking at it and wasn't going to touch it; he might have tried
to persuade her that it was indeed the right thing to do, to try
changing its adjustment. All of these responses take the anger
on by directly responding to the claims implicit in it: accepting them or challenging them, accepting or defending himself
against the implicit charge or accusation. He did not meet the
anger and its claims. He moved to a different level. What he
did was irrelevant. He changed the subject—from the matter
of his actions and the carburetor to the matter of her character and sanity. He did not give her anger uptake.

Deprived of uptake, the woman's anger is left as just a
burst of expression of individual feeling. As a social act, an
act of communication, it just doesn't happen. It is, as Austin
would have said, "non-played."

The sort of uncooperativeness displayed by the gas station
attendant is a rejection of anger's claims. It rejects them not
simply as arguably false or unjustified, but as claims so wildly
and obviously off the mark as to confound response. It rejects them as claims only someone in an abnormal state—hysterical or mad—could make; as implying accusations so obviously fantastic that they could be motivated only by a
fevered and indiscriminate malice. The claimant can only be
a crazy bitch.

One's anger presupposes certain things about what sort of
being one is and what sorts of relations are possible between

---

* For those who do not know about carburetors: This organ of the
gasoline engine mixes gasoline and air (oxygen) in just the right proportions to enable the gasoline to ignite and to burn efficiently. Getting it
properly adjusted is a delicate and often frustrating job, and its maladjustment causes all sorts of trouble. When you've got it right, you don't
touch it; and even when you suspect it is not right, it is the last thing
you experiment with in your diagnostic efforts.

oneself and another. The patterns of claims someone can and cannot countenance, of the acts one can and cannot give uptake to, is a partial map of one's world view. It reveals something of one's understanding of the essential natures and relations of things.

You say the movie is at 7:30 and I disagree, saying it is at 7:00. I am puzzled by your getting it wrong, since I think you must have phoned the theater, just as I did. But we are still in the same world of belief and discourse. Another day, you say you are the messiah and I should worship you. This situation is rather different. I don't know how to argue with you about that (assuming I am satisfied that we mean the same things by these words). I have certain understandings of what a messiah would be if there were one, of what worship is, and of the circumstances under which worship might be appropriate. These are enmeshed far more deeply in my basic understanding of the world than is my confidence in the health of any one particular human being I may encounter. As I understand this world, human individuals run amok far more often than messiahs appear, if they ever do. If I am convinced that you are serious, I can only suppose there is, in some sense, something wrong with you.

To get angry is to claim implicitly that one is a certain sort of being, a being which can (and in this case does) stand in a certain relation and position *a propos* the being one is angry at. One claims that one is in certain ways and dimensions *respectable*. One makes claims upon respect. For any woman to presuppose any such thing of herself is at best potentially problematic and at worst incomprehensible in the world of male-supremacy where women are Women and men are Men. A man's concept of Woman and of Man, and his understanding of what sorts of relations and connections are possible between beings of these sorts, to a great extent determine the range of his capacity to comprehend these claims, and hence of his capacity to give uptake to women's anger.

In some cases women can get angry without much risk of being thought crazy, hushed up or beaten up. Usually, women can get angry at children, or in behalf of children. A woman may get away with being angry at some oaf who slammed a door and thus ruined her souffle, or at another who disarranged the pages of a report she has typed and is collating. On the other hand, she is not likely to get away with being angry at the oaf who maladjusts her carbuertor. The pattern is obvious. Kids, homemaking and secretarial service belong to women; cars belong to men. So long as a woman is operating squarely within a realm which is generally recognized as a woman's realm, labeled as such by stereotypes of women and of certain activities, her anger will quite likely be tolerated, at least not thought crazy. It seems to me that in general, if a woman's purposive behavior and the web of interests and authority it weaves can be seen as falling within the place and functions of Mother/Caretaker/Conserver/Helpmate, her claim to authority, interest, presence and place will make sense to relevant others. It is likely to accord well enough with their concept of Woman.*

We are indebted to women of the nineteenth century for extending the range of tolerance of women's anger. The struggles and victories of abolitionists, suffragists, prohibitionists and other reformers made it relatively safe for women to get angry, publicly, in behalf of great moral causes. Generally speaking, women can get angry about such things as nuclear energy and arms, pollution, war, starving children or drunken driving. (This does not mean, still, that we are so likely to be taken very seriously. Our anger is likely to be perceived as "understandable, but ill-informed.")

---

* Often a woman's anger, even when she is within this range of social places, will not be taken particularly seriously, but that is because all that belongs in this range of social places is likely to be thought trivial. Not being taken seriously is not quite the same as being thought mad. Still, if the woman insists persistently enough on her anger being taken seriously, she may begin to seem mad, for she will seem to have her values all mixed up and distorted.

This extension, hard won as it was, represents only a relatively small shift in the concept of Woman. Historically and logically it was an extension of our "right" to mother. We can be relatively easily perceived as mothers to our nations or to our peoples (which in some cases are imaged in dominant mythology as childlike), or to the species. By virtue of this, we can be understood if we claim legitimate interest and some degree of authority in the matter of their protection and preservation.* Also, as an extension of mothering into matters of public welfare, it still permits women's anger only *in behalf of others,* not in our own behalves.

A woman's anger on another's behalf is far more likely to get uptake, and even acceptance, than her anger in her own behalf. This is why it is easier for a woman to be passionately anti-abortion than passionately "pro-choice." One is within the bounds of concepts of Woman which are more widely shared and more warmly sanctioned when one's passion is in defense of others (especially if the others can plausibly be presented as "innocent" and as "children" or "babies"). For the same sorts of reasons, women's claims to some sort of propriety and authority in our interest in "peace" and "the survival of humanity" are generally more credible in this culture than women's claims to a like propriety and authority in our interests in our own skins, genitals or wombs. Hence it is safer to get angry about nuclear power than about one's own rape; the former is more likely to be intelligible, to get uptake.

To expand the scope of one's intelligible anger is to change one's place in the universe, to change another's concept of what one is, to become something different in that social and collective scheme which determines the limits of the intelligible. Nineteenth century women succeeded in expanding the

---

* I have considerable respect for mothering and believe that the attitudes and practices of good mothering can make a very valuable contribution to the conduct of things in the sphere of public politics and morality. Things will have changed more, and more for the better, when we can mother as appropriate without being seen as Mothers, and can, as women, do a great deal else as well.

concept of Woman, that is, really, the concept of Mother, to the point where a woman could express anger in a public matter and be found intelligible. Contemporary feminists have taken on the more radical project of expanding the concept of Woman to the point where a woman can assert herself and make demands upon respect, in public or private, simply in her own behalf. Not, that is, as any kind or degree of Mother, but simply as a being, herself, worthy of respect.

Not all anger is justified, and as long as we have concepts of ourselves, others and the relations amongst us, some anger will sometimes be unintelligible. And of course others' concepts of us are not always objectionable. Different men, and indeed different women, differ in detail in what concept they have of Woman, and what they would or could perceive as "a woman going about her business, pursuing her interests, by means and using resources which are properly hers to employ." Some men, for instance, think all affairs pertaining to birth control are entirely "female" concerns and virtue requires of men who engage sexually with women only that they let women take care of it. But also, some husbands think a wife's fecundity is entirely the husband's to control and manage. The first sort of man would be baffled by a woman's anger at his not taking any responsibility; the second sort would be baffled by his wife's anger at his getting her pregnant. In both cases, the discovery of what baffles is the discovery of some aspect of what the man thinks a woman is.

No two women live, in a daily and detailed way, in identical spaces created by identical ranges of concepts of Woman. Some of us, indeed, have consciously constructed situations for ourselves in which we will be shaped by chosen and wholesome concepts of Woman. For better or for worse though, in each of our lives, others' concepts of us are revealed by the limits of the intelligibility of our anger. Anger can be an instrument of cartography. By determining where, with whom, about what and in what circumstances one can get angry and get uptake, one can map others' concepts of who and what one is.

One woman took this thought home with her and tried it out. She walked about the apartment she shared, not unhappily, with her young husband, testing in imagination for the viability of her anger—in what situations it would "work," would get uptake. She discovered the pattern was very simple and clear. It went with the floor plan. She could get angry quite freely in the kitchen and somewhat less freely and about a more limited range of things in the living room. She could not get angry in the bedroom.

Anger. Domain. Respect.

NOTES

1. See "Getting Angry," by Susi Kaplow, and "Men and Violence," a transcript of a taped consciousness-raising session, in *Radical Feminism*, edited by Anne Koedt, Ellen Levine and Anita Rapone (Quadrangle, New York, 1973).

2. See "Rape and Respect," by Carolyn Shafer and Marilyn Frye, in *Feminism and Philosophy*, edited by Mary Vetterling-Braggin, Frederick A. Elliston and Jane English (Littlefield, Adams & Co., Totowa, New Jersey, 1977).

3. J.L. Austin, *How To Do Things With Words* (Oxford University Press, 1962).

SOME REFLECTIONS ON SEPARATISM AND POWER*

I have been trying to write something about separatism almost since my first dawning of feminist consciousness, but it has always been for me somehow a mercurial topic which, when I tried to grasp it, would softly shatter into many other topics like sexuality, man-hating, so-called reverse discrimination, apocalyptic utopianism, and so on. What I have to share with you today is my latest attempt to get to the heart of the matter.

In my life, and within feminism as I understand it, separatism is not a theory or a doctrine, nor a demand for certain specific behaviors on the part of feminists, though it is undeniably connected with lesbianism. Feminism seems to me to be kaleidoscopic—something whose shapes, structures and patterns alter with every turn of feminist creativity; and one

---

* This paper was first presented at a meeting of the Society for Women in Philosophy, Eastern Division, in December of 1977. It was first printed in *Sinister Wisdom 6*, Summer, 1978. It is also available as a pamphlet from Tea Rose Press, P.O. Box 591, East Lansing, Michigan, 48823. Before it was published, I received many helpful comments from those who heard or read the paper. I have incorporated some, made notes of others. I got help from Carolyn Shafer in seeing the structure of it all, in particular, the connections among parasitism, access and definition.

element which is present through all the changes is an element
of separation. This element has different roles and relations
in different turns of the glass—it assumes different meanings,
is variously conspicuous, variously determined or determining,
depending on how the pieces fall and who is the beholder.
The theme of separation, in its multitude variations, is there
in everything from divorce to exclusive lesbian separatist communities, from shelters for battered women to witch covens,
from women's studies programs to women's bars, from expansion of daycare to abortion on demand. The presence of this
theme is vigorously obscured, trivialized, mystified and outright denied by many feminist apologists, who seem to find it
embarrassing, while it is embraced, explored, expanded and
ramified by most of the more inspiring theorists and activists.
The theme of separation is noticeably absent or heavily qualified in most of the things I take to be personal solutions and
band-aid projects, like legalization of prostitution, liberal marriage contracts, improvement of the treatment of rape victims
and affirmative action. It is clear to me, in my own case at
least, that the contrariety of assimilation and separation is
one of the main things that guides or determines assessments
of various theories, actions and practices as reformist or radical, as going to the root of the thing or being relatively superficial. So my topical question comes to this: What is it about
separation, in any or all of its many forms and degrees, that
makes it so basic and so sinister, so exciting and so repellent?

Feminist separation is, of course, separation of various sorts
or modes from men and from institutions, relationships, roles
and activities which are male-defined, male-dominated and operating for the benefit of males and the maintenance of male
privilege—this separation being initiated or maintained, at will,
by women. (Masculist separatism is the partial segregation of
women from men and male domains *at the will of men.* This
difference is crucial.) The feminist separation can take many

forms. Breaking up or avoiding close relationships or working relationships; forbidding someone to enter your house; excluding someone from your company, or from your meeting; withdrawal from participation in some activity or institution, or avoidance of participation; avoidance of communications and influence from certain quarters (not listening to music with sexist lyrics, not watching tv); withholding commitment or support; rejection of or rudeness toward obnoxious individuals.* Some separations are subtle realignments of identification, priorities and commitments, or working with agendas which only incidently coincide with the agendas of the institution one works in.¹ Ceasing to be loyal to something or someone is a separation; and ceasing to love. The feminist's separations are rarely if ever sought or maintained directly as ultimate personal or political ends. The closest we come to that, I think, is the separation which is the instinctive and self-preserving recoil from the systematic misogyny that surrounds us.** Generally, the separations are brought about and maintained for the sake of something else like independence, liberty, growth, invention, sisterhood, safety, health, or the practice of novel or heretical customs.² Often the separations in question evolve, unpremeditated, as one goes one's way and finds various persons, institutions or relationships useless, obstructive or noisome and leaves them aside or behind. Sometimes the separations are consciously planned and cultivated

---

* *Adrienne Rich: "...makes me question the whole idea of 'courtesy' or 'rudeness'—surely their constructs, since women become 'rude' when we ignore or reject male obnoxiousness, while male 'rudeness' is usually punctuated with the 'Haven't you a sense of humor' tactic."* Yes; me too. I embrace rudeness; our compulsive/compulsory politeness so often is what coerces us into their "fellowship."

** *Ti-Grace Atkinson: Should give more attention here to our vulnerability to assault and degradation, and to separation as protection.* Okay, but then we have to re-emphasize that it has to be separation at *our* behest—we've had enough of their imposed separation for our "protection." (There's no denying that in my real-life life, protection and maintenance of places for healing are major motives for separation.)

as necessary prerequisites or conditions for getting on with one's business. Sometimes the separations are accomplished or maintained easily, or with a sense of relief, or even joy; sometimes they are accomplished or maintained with difficulty, by dint of constant vigilance, or with anxiety, pain or grief.

Most feminists, probably all, practice some separation from males and male-dominated institutions. A separatist practices separation consciously, systematically, and probably more generally than the others, and advocates thorough and "broad-spectrum" separation as part of the conscious strategy of liberation. And, contrary to the image of the separatist as a cowardly escapist,[3] hers is the life and program which inspires the greatest hostility, disparagement, insult and confrontation and generally she is the one against whom economic sanctions operate most conclusively. The penalty for refusing to work with or for men is usually starvation (or, at the very least, doing without medical insurance[4]); and if one's policy of noncooperation is more subtle, one's livelihood is still constantly on the line, since one is not a loyal partisan, a proper member of the team, or what have you. The penalties for being a lesbian are ostracism, harassment and job insecurity or joblessness. The penalty for rejecting men's sexual advances is often rape and, perhaps even more often, forfeit of such things as professional or job opportunities. And the separatist lives with the added burden of being assumed by many to be a morally depraved man-hating bigot. But there is a clue here: if you are doing something that is so strictly forbidden by the patriarchs, you must be doing something right.

There is an idea floating around in both feminist and anti-feminist literature to the effect that females and males generally live in a relation of parasitism,[5] a parasitism of the male on the female. . .that it is, generally speaking, the strength, energy, inspiration and nurturance of women that keeps men going, and not the strength, aggression, spirituality and hunting of men that keeps women going.

It is sometimes said that the parasitism goes the other way around, that the female is the parasite. But one can conjure the appearance of the female as parasite only if one takes a very narrow view of human living—historically parochial, narrow with respect to class and race, and limited in conception of what are the necessary goods. Generally, the female's contribution to her material support is and always has been substantial; in many times and places it has been independently sufficient. One can and should distinguish between a partial and contingent material dependence created by a certain sort of money economy and class structure, and the nearly ubiquitous spiritual, emotional and material dependence of males on females. Males presently provide, off and on, a portion of the material support of women, within circumstances apparently designed to make it difficult for women to provide them for themselves. But females provide and generally have provided for males the energy and spirit for living; the males are nurtured by the females. And this the males apparently cannot do for themselves, even partially.

The parasitism of males on females is, as I see it, demonstrated by the panic, rage and hysteria generated in so many of them by the thought of being abandoned by women. But it is demonstrated in a way that is perhaps more generally persuasive by both literary and sociological evidence. Evidence cited in Jesse Bernard's work in *The Future of Marriage* and in George Gilder's *Sexual Suicide* and *Men Alone* convincingly shows that males tend in shockingly significant numbers and in alarming degree to fall into mental illness, petty crime, alcoholism, physical infirmity, chronic unemployment, drug addiction and neurosis when deprived of the care and companionship of a female mate, or keeper. (While on the other hand, women without male mates are significantly healthier and happier than women with male mates.) And masculist literature is abundant with indications of male cannibalism,

of males deriving essential sustenance from females. Canni-
balistic imagery, visual and verbal, is common in pornography:
images likening women to food, and sex to eating. And, as
documented in Millett's *Sexual Politics* and many other feminist analyses of masculist literature, the theme of men getting
high off beating, raping or killing women (or merely bullying
them) is common. These interactions with women, or rather,
these actions upon women, make men feel good, walk tall,
feel refreshed, in*vigor*ated. Men are drained and depleted by
their living by themselves and with and among other men, and
are revived and refreshed, re-created, by going home and being served dinner, changing to clean clothes, having sex with
the wife; or by dropping by the apartment of a woman friend
to be served coffee or a drink and stroked in one way or another; or by picking up a prostitute for a quicky or for a dip
in favorite sexual escape fantasies; or by raping refugees from
their wars (foreign and domestic). The ministrations of wom-
en, be they willing or unwilling, free or paid for, are what re-
store in men the strength, will and confidence to go on with
what they call living.

   If it is true that a fundamental aspect of the relations between the sexes is male parasitism, it might help to explain
why certain issues are particularly exciting to patriarchal loyalists. For instance, in view of the obvious advantages of
easy abortion to population control, to control of welfare
rolls, and to ensuring sexual availability of women to men,
it is a little surprising that the loyalists are so adamant and
riled up in their objection to it. But look. . .

   The fetus lives parasitically. It is a distinct animal surviving
off the life (the blood) of another animal creature. It is incapable of surviving on its own resources, of independent nutrition; incapable even of symbiosis. If it is true that males
live parasitically upon females, it seems reasonable to suppose
that many of them and those loyal to them are in some way
sensitive to the parallelism between their situation and that of
the fetus. They could easily identify with the fetus. The

woman who is free to see the fetus as a parasite* might be free to see the man as a parasite. The woman's willingness to cut off the life line to one parasite suggests a willingness to cut off the life line to another parasite. The woman who is capable (legally, psychologically, physically) of decisively, self-interestedly, independently rejecting the one parasite, is capable of rejecting, with the same decisiveness and independence, the like burden of the other parasite. In the eyes of the other parasite, the image of the wholly self-determined abortion, involving not even a ritual submission to male veto power, is the mirror image of death.

Another clue here is that one line of argument against free and easy abortion is the slippery slope argument that if fetuses are to be freely dispensed with, old people will be next. Old people? Why are old people next? And why the great concern for them? Most old people are women, indeed, and patriarchal loyalists are not generally so solicitous of the welfare of any women. Why old people? Because, I think, in the modern patriarchal divisions of labor, old people too are parasites on women. The anti-abortion folks seem not to worry about wife beating and wife murder—there is no broad or emotional popular support for stopping these violences. They do not worry about murder and involuntary sterilization in prisons, nor murder in war, nor murder by pollution and industrial accidents. Either these are not real to them or they cannot identify with the victims; but anyway, killing in general is not what they oppose. They worry about the rejection *by women, at women's discretion,* of something which lives parasitically on women. I suspect that they fret not because old people are next, but because men are next.

---

* *Caroline Whitbeck: Cross-cultural evidence suggests it's not the fetus that gets rejected in cultures where abortion is common, it is the role of motherhood, the burden, in particular, of "illegitimacy"; where the institution of illegitimacy does not exist, abortion rates are pretty low.* This suggests to me that the woman's rejection of the fetus is even more directly a rejection of the male and his world than I had thought.

There are other reasons, of course, why patriarchal loyalists should be disturbed about abortion on demand; a major one being that it would be a significant form of female control of reproduction, and at least from certain angles it looks like the progress of patriarchy *is* the progress toward male control of reproduction, starting with possession of wives and continuing through the invention of obstetrics and the technology of extrauterine gestation. Giving up that control would be giving up patriarchy. But such an objection to abortion is too abstract, and requires too historical a vision, to generate the hysteria there is now in the reaction against abortion. The hysteria is, I think, to be accounted for more in terms of a much more immediate and personal presentiment of ejection by the woman-womb.[6]

I discuss abortion here because it seems to me to be the most publicly emotional and most physically dramatic ground on which the theme of separation and male parasitism is presently being played out. But there are other locales for this play. For instance,[7] women with newly raised consciousnesses tend to leave marriages and families, either completely through divorce, or partially, through unavailability of their cooking, housekeeping and sexual services. And women academics tend to become alienated from their colleagues and male mentors and no longer serve as sounding board, ego booster, editor, mistress or proofreader. Many awakening women become celibate or lesbian, and the others become a very great deal more choosy about when, where and in what relationships they will have sex with men. And the men affected by these separations generally react with defensive hostility, anxiety and guilt-tripping, not to mention descents into illogical argument which match and exceed their own most fanciful images of female irrationality. My claim is that they are very afraid because they depend very heavily upon the goods they receive from women, and these separations cut them off from those goods.

Male parasitism means that males *must have access* to women; it is the Patriarchal Imperative. But feminist no-saying is more than a substantial removal (redirection, reallocation) of goods and services because Access is one of the faces of Power. Female denial of male access to females substantially cuts off a flow of benefits, but it has also the form and full portent of assumption of power.

Differences of power are always manifested in asymmetrical access. The President of the United States has access to almost everybody for almost anything he might want of them, and almost nobody has access to him. The super-rich have access to almost everybody; almost nobody has access to them. The resources of the employee are available to the boss as the resources of the boss are not to the employee. The parent has unconditional access to the child's room; the child does not have similar access to the parent's room. Students adjust to professors' office hours; professors do not adjust to students' conference hours. The child is required not to lie; the parent is free to close out the child with lies at her discretion. The slave is unconditionally accessible to the master. Total power is unconditional access; total powerlessness is being unconditionally accessible. The creation and manipulation of power is constituted of the manipulation and control of access.

All-woman groups, meetings, projects seem to be great things for causing controversy and confrontation. Many women are offended by them; many are afraid to be the one to announce the exclusion of men; it is seen as a device whose use needs much elaborate justification. I think this is because conscious and deliberate exclusion of men by women, from anything, is blatant insubordination, and generates in women fear of punishment and reprisal (fear which is often well-justified). Our own timidity and desire to avoid confrontations generally keep us from doing very much in the way of all-woman groups and meetings. But when we do, we invariably run into the male champion who challenges our right to do it. Only a small minority of men go crazy when an event is advertised to be for women only—just one man tried to crash our women-only Rape Speak-Out, and only a few hid under the auditorium seats to try to spy on a women-only meeting at a NOW convention in Philadelphia. But these few are onto something their less rabid com-patriots are missing. The woman-only meeting is a fundamental challenge to the structure of power. It is always the privilege of the master to enter the slave's hut. The slave who decides to exclude the master from her hut is declaring herself not a slave. The exclusion of men from the meeting not only deprives them of certain benefits (which they might survive without); it is a controlling of access, hence an assumption of power. It is not only mean, it is arrogant.

It becomes clearer now why there is always an off-putting aura of negativity about separatism—one which offends the feminine pollyanna in us and smacks of the purely defensive to the political theorist in us. It is this: First: When those who control access have made you totally accessible, your first act of taking control must be denying access, or must have denial of access as one of its aspects. This is not because you are charged up with (unfeminine or politically incorrect) negativity; it is because of the logic of the situation. When we start from a position of total accessibility there *must* be an aspect of no-saying (which is the beginning of control) in *every effective* act and strategy, the effective ones being precisely those which *shift power,* i.e., ones which involve manipulation and control of access. Second: Whether or not one says "no," or withholds or closes out or rejects, on this occasion or that, the capacity and ability to say "no" (with effect) is logically necessary to control. When we are in control of access to ourselves there will be some no-saying, and when we are more accustomed to it, when it is more common, an ordinary part of living, it will not seem so prominent, obvious, or strained. . .we will not strike ourselves or others as being particularly negative. In this aspect of ourselves and our lives, we will strike ourselves pleasingly as active beings with momentum of our own, with sufficient shape and structure—with sufficient integrity—to generate friction. Our experience of our no-saying will be an aspect of our experience of our definition.

When our feminist acts or practices have an aspect of separation, we are assuming power by controlling access and simultaneously by undertaking definition. The slave who excludes the master from her hut thereby declares herself *not a slave.* And *definition* is another face of power.

The powerful normally determine what is said and sayable. When the powerful label something or dub it or baptize it, the thing becomes what they call it. When the Secretary of Defense calls something a peace negotiation, for instance, then whatever it is that he called a peace negotiation is an instance of negotiating peace. If the activity in question is the working out of terms of a trade-off of nuclear reactors and territorial redistributions, complete with arrangements for the resulting refugees, that is peacemaking. People laud it, and the negotiators get Noble Piece Prizes for it. On the other hand, when I call a certain speech act a rape, my "calling" it does not make it so. At best, I have to explain and justify and make clear exactly what it is about this speech act which is assaultive in just what way, and then the others acquiesce in saying the act was *like* rape or could figuratively be called a rape. My counterassault will not be counted a simple case of self-defense. And what I called rejection of parasitism, they call the loss of the womanly virtues of compassion and "caring." And generally, when renegade women call something one thing and patriarchal loyalists call it another, the loyalists get their way.*

_____

* This paragraph and the succeeding one are the passage which has provoked the most substantial questions from women who read the paper. One thing that causes trouble here is that I am talking from a stance or position that is ambiguous—it is located in two different and noncommunicating systems of thought-action. *Re* the patriarchy and the English language, there is general usage over which I/we do not have the

Women generally are not the people who do the defining, and we cannot from our isolation and powerlessness simply commence saying different things than others say and make it stick. There is a humpty-dumpty problem in that. But we are able to arrogate definition to ourselves when we re-pattern access. Assuming control of access, we draw new boundaries and create new roles and relationships. This, though it causes some strain, puzzlement and hostility, is to a fair extent within the scope of individuals and small gangs, as outright verbal redefinition is not, at least in the first instance.

One may see access as coming in two sorts, "natural" and humanly arranged. A grizzly bear has what you might call natural access to the picnic basket of the unarmed human. The access of the boss to the personal services of the secretary is humanly arranged access; the boss exercises institutional power. It looks to me, looking from a certain angle, like institutions *are* humanly designed patterns of access—

---

control that elite males have (with the cooperation of all the ordinary patriarchal loyalists). *Re* the new being and meaning which are being created now by lesbian-feminists, we *do* have semantic authority, and, collectively, can and do define with effect. I think it is only by maintaining our boundaries through controlling concrete access to us that we can enforce on those who are not-us our definitions of ourselves, hence force on them *the fact of our existence* and thence open up the *possibility* of our having semantic authority with them. (I wrote some stuff that's relevant to this in the last section of my paper "Male Chauvinism— A Conceptual Analysis.")[8] Our unintelligibility to patriarchal loyalists is a source of pride and delight, in some contexts; but if we don't have an effect on their usage while we continue, willy nilly, to be subject to theirs, being totally unintelligible to them could be fatal. (A friend of mine had a dream where the women were meeting in a cabin at the edge of town, and they had a sort of inspiration through the vision of one of them that they should put a sign on the door which would connect with the patriarchs' meaning-system, for otherwise the men would be too curious/frightened about them and would break the door down to get in. They put a picture of a fish on the door.) Of course, you might say that *being* intelligible to them might be fatal. Well, perhaps it's best to be in a position to make tactical decisions about when and how to be intelligible and unintelligible.

access to persons and their services. But institutions are artifacts of definition. In the case of intentionally and formally designed institutions, this is very clear, for the relevant definitions are explicitly set forth in by-laws and constitutions, regulations and rules. When one defines the term "president," one defines presidents in terms of what they can do and what is owed them by other offices, and "what they can do" is a matter of their access to the services of others. Similarly, definitions of *dean, student, judge,* and *cop* set forth patterns of access, and definitions of *writer, child, owner,* and of course, *husband, wife,* and *man* and *girl.* When one changes the pattern of access, one forces new uses of words on those affected. The term 'man' has to shift in meaning when rape is no longer possible. When we take control of sexual access to us, of access to our nurturance and to our reproductive function, access to mothering and sistering, we redefine the word 'woman.' The shift of usage is pressed on others by a change in social reality; it does not await their recognition of our definitional authority.

When women separate (withdraw, break out, regroup, transcend, shove aside, step outside, migrate, say *no*), we are simultaneously controlling access and defining. We are doubly insubordinate, since neither of these is permitted. And access and definition are fundamental ingredients in the alchemy of power, so we are doubly, and radically, insubordinate.

If these, then, are some of the ways in which separation is at the heart of our struggle, it helps to explain why separation is such a hot topic. If there is one thing women are queasy about it is *actually taking power.* As long as one stops just short of that, the patriarchs will for the most part take an indulgent attitude. We are afraid of what will happen to us when we really frighten them. This is not an irrational fear. It is our experience in the movement generally that the defensiveness, nastiness, violence, hostility and irrationality of the reaction to feminism tends to correlate with the blatancy of the element of separation in the strategy or project which triggers the reaction. The separations involved in women leaving homes, marriages and boyfriends, separations from fetuses, and the separation of lesbianism are all pretty dramatic. That is, they are dramatic and blatant when perceived from within the framework provided by the patriarchal world view and male parasitism. Matters pertaining to marriage and divorce, lesbianism and abortion touch individual men (and their sympathizers) because they can feel the relevance of these to themselves—they can feel the threat that they might be the next. Hence, heterosexuality, marriage and motherhood, which are the institutions which most obviously and individually maintain female accessibility to males, form the core triad of antifeminist ideology; and all-woman spaces, all-woman organizations, all-woman meetings, all-woman classes, are outlawed, suppressed, harassed, ridiculed and punished—in the name of that other fine and enduring patriarchal institution, Sex Equality.

To some of us these issues can seem almost foreign. . . strange ones to be occupying center stage. We are busily engaged in what seem to *us* our blatant insubordinations: living our own lives, taking care of ourselves and one another, doing our work, and in particular, telling it as we see it. Still, the original sin is the separation which these presuppose, and it is that, not our art or philosophy, not our speechmaking, nor our "sexual acts" (or abstinences), for which we will be persecuted, when worse comes to worst.

NOTES

1. Help from Claudia Card.

2. Help from Chris Pierce and Sara Ann Ketchum. See "Separatism and Sexual Relationships," in *A Philosophical Approach to Women's Liberation*, eds. S. Hill and M. Weinzweig (Wadsworth, Belmont, California, 1978).

3. Answering Claudia Card.

4. Levity due to Carolyn Shafer.

5. I first noticed this when reading *Beyond God the Father*, by Mary Daly (Beacon Press, Boston, 1973). See also *Women's Evolution*, by Evelyn Reed (Pathfinder Press, New York, 1975) for rich hints about male cannibalism and male dependence.

6. Claudia Card.

7. The instances mentioned are selected for their relevance to the lives of the particular women addressed in this talk. There are many other sorts of instances to be drawn from other sorts of women's lives.

8. In (improbably enough) *Philosophy and Sex*, edited by Robert Baker and Frederick Elliston (Prometheus Books, Buffalo, New York, 1976).

ON BEING WHITE: THINKING TOWARD A FEMINIST UNDERSTANDING OF RACE AND RACE SUPREMACY*

I

White feminists come to renewed and earnest thought about racism not entirely spontaneously. We are pressed by women of color. Women of color have been at feminist conferences, meetings and festivals and speaking up, pointing out that their needs and interests are not being taken into account nor answered and that much that white feminists do and say is racist. Some white feminists have been aware of and acting

* This is a slightly revised version of the text of a talk I delivered to a general audience at Cornell University, sponsored by the Women's Studies Program, the Philosophy Department and the James H. Becker Alumni Lecture Series, October 29, 1981. In the revision process I profited from the comments and criticisms of Nancy Bereano, Michelle Cliff, Michele Nevels, Carolyn Shafer, Sandra Siegel, Sharon Tuttle and Dorothy Yoshimuri. This piece, more than any other in the collection, directly reflects and is limited by my own location, both culturally and in a process of change. The last thing I would want is that it be read either as my last, or as a complete, account of what whiteness is and of what that means to a white feminist. I do not for a moment take it or intend it to be either.

against racism all along, and spontaneously, but the topic of racism has arrived per force in the feminist newspapers and journals, at the National Women's Studies Association, in women's centers and women's bookstores in the last couple of years, not so much because some white feminists urged this but because women of color have demanded it.

Nonetheless, many white feminists have to a fair extent *responded* to the demand; by which I mean, white feminists have to a fair extent chosen to *hear* what it was usually in their power not to hear. The hearing is, as anyone who has been on the scene knows, sometimes very defensive, sometimes dulled by fear, sometimes alarmingly partial or distorted. But it has interested me that I and other white feminists have heard the objections and demands, for I think it is an aspect of race privilege to have a choice—a choice between the options of hearing and not hearing. That is part of what being white gets you.

This matter of the powers white feminists have because of being white came up for me very concretely in a real-life situation a while back. Conscientiously, and with the encouragement of various women of color—both friends and women speaking in the feminist press—a group of white women formed a white women's consciousness-raising group to identify and explore the racism in our lives with a view to dismantling the barriers that blocked our understanding and action in this matter. As is obvious from this description, we certainly thought of ourselves as doing the right thing. Some women of color talked with us about their view that it was racist to make it a group for white women *only;* we discussed our reasons and invited women of color who wanted to participate to come to the meeting for further discussion.

In a later community meeting, one Black woman criticized us very angrily for ever thinking we could achieve our goals by working only with white women. We said we never meant this few weeks of this particular kind of work to be *all* we ever did and told her we had decided at the beginning to organize a group open to all women shortly after our series of white women's meetings came to a close. Well, as some of you will know without my telling, we could hardly have said anything less satisfying to our critic. She exploded with rage: "*You* decided!" Yes. We consulted the opinions of some women of color, but still, we decided. "Isn't that what we are supposed to do?" we said to ourselves, "Take responsibility, decide what to do, and do something?" She seemed to be enraged by our making decisions, by our acting, by our doing anything. It seemed like doing nothing would be racist and whatever we did would be racist just because *we* did it. We began to lose hope; we felt bewildered and trapped. It seemed that what our critic was saying must be right; but what she was saying didn't seem to make any sense.

She seemed crazy to me.

That stopped me.

I paused and touched and weighed that seeming. It was familiar. I know it as deceptive, defensive. I know it from both sides; I have been thought crazy by others too righteous, too timid and too defended to grasp the enormity of our difference and the significance of their offenses. I backed off. To get my balance, I reached for what I knew when I was not frightened.

A woman was called "schizophrenic." She said her father was trying to kill her. He was beside himself: anguished and baffled that she would not drink coffee he brought her for fear he had poisoned it. How could she think that? But then, why had she "gone mad" and been reduced to incompetence by the ensuing familial and social processes? Was her father trying to kill her? No, of course not: he was a good-willed man and loved his daughter. But also, yes, of course. Every good fatherly thing about him, including his caring decisions about what will improve things for her, are poisonous to her. The Father is death to The Daughter. And she knows it.

What is it that our Black woman critic knows? Am I racist when I (a white woman) decide what I shall do to try to grow and heal the wounds and scars of racism among lesbians and feminists? Am I racist if I decide to do nothing? If I decide to refuse to work with other white women on our racism? My deciding, deciding anything, is poison to her. Is this what she knows?

Every choice or decision I make is made in a matrix of options. Racism distorts and limits that matrix in various ways. My being on the white side of racism leaves me a different variety of options than are available to a woman of color. As a white woman I have certain freedoms and liberties. When I use them, according to my white woman's judgment, to act on matters of racism, my enterprise reflects strangely on the matrix of options within which it is undertaken. In the case at hand, I was deciding when to relate to white women and when to relate to women of color according to what I thought would reduce my racism, enhance my growth and improve my politics. It becomes clearer why no decision I make here can fail to be an exercise of race privilege. (And yet this cannot be an excuse for not making a decision, though perhaps it suggests that a decision should be made at a different level.)

Does being white make it impossible for me to be a good person?

II

What is this "being white" that gets me into so much trouble, after so many years of seeming to me to be so benign? What is this privilege of race? What is race?

First, there is the matter of skin color. Supposedly one is white if one is white. I mean, one is a member of the white race if one's skin is white. But that is not really so. Many people whose skin is white, by which of course we don't really mean *white,* are Black or Mexican or Puerto Rican or Mohawk. And some people who are dark-skinned are white. Natives of India and Pakistan are generally counted as white in this country though perhaps to the average white American they look dark. While it cannot be denied that conceptions of race and of whiteness have much to do with fetishes about pigmentation, that seems to me not to be the Heart of Whiteness. Light skin may get a person *counted* as white; it does not make a person white.

Whiteness is, it seems pretty obvious, a social or political construct of some sort, something elaborated upon conceptions of kinship or common ancestry and upon ancient ethnocentric associations of good and evil with light and dark. Those who fashion this construct of whiteness, who elaborate on these conceptions, are primarily a certain group of males. It is *their* construct. They construct a conception of their "us," their kindred, their nation, their tribe. Earliest uses of the word 'race' in English, according to *The Oxford English Dictionary,* make this clear. The people of one's race were those of a common lineage or ancestry. People of like coloring could be of different races. The connection of race to color was a historical development and one which did not entirely eclipse the earlier meaning. Race, as defined and conceived by the white male arbiters of conceptions, is still not entirely a matter of color. One can be very pale, and yet if there are persons of color in one's lineage, one can be classed as Black, Indian, etc.

On the other hand, it is the experience of light-skinned people from family and cultural backgrounds that are Black or another dark group that white people tend to disbelieve or discount their tellings of their histories. There is a pressure coming from white people to make light-skinned people be white. Michelle Cliff speaks of this in her book *Claiming An Identity They Taught Me To Despise.*[1] Cliff is a light-skinned woman who looks white to most white people. She encounters among white people resistance, even hostility, to her assertion that she is Black. In another case, a friend of mine to whom I have been quite close off and on for some fifteen or twenty years, noticed I was assuming she is white: she told me she had told me years ago that she is Mexican. Apparently I did not hear, or I forgot, or it was convenient for me to *white-wash* her.*

The concept of whiteness is not just used, in these cases, it is *wielded*. Whites exercise a power of defining who is white and who is not, and are jealous of that power.[2] If a light-skinned person of "colored" kinship claims to be white, and white people discover the person's background, they see that a person who might be a marginal case has *decided* what she is. Because the white person cannot allow that deciding, the decision must be reversed. On the other hand, when someone has been clearly and definitively decided to be white *by* whites, her claim that she is *not* white must be challenged; again because anyone who is even possibly marginal cannot be allowed to draw the line. To such a person, a white person is saying: I have decided you are white so you are white, because what I say about who is white and who is not is definitive.

To be white is to be a member of an in-group, a kin group, which is self-defining. Just as with fraternities or sororities, the power to draw the membership line is jealously guarded. Though a variety of traits and histories are relevant to whether one will be defined into or out of that group, one essential thing is that the group is self-defining, that it exercises control of access to membership. Members can bend the rules of membership anytime, if that is necessary to assert the members' sole and exclusive authority to *decide* who is a member; in fact, bending the rules is an ideal expression of that authority.

A particularly insidious expression of this emerges when members of the self-appointed "superior" group tend casually to grant membership by "generously" giving people "the

---

* As Ran Hall pointed out: "the definition of 'whitewash'—a concealing or glossing over of flaws—does not imply improving or correcting an object or situation but the covering of reality with a cheap, inferior disguise (whiteness)." See "dear martha," in *Common Lives Lesbian Lives: A Lesbian Quarterly*, No. 6., Winter, 1982, p. 40.

benefit of the doubt." If the question does not arise, or does not arise explicitly or blatantly, one will generally be assumed by white people to be white, since the contrary assumption might be (by white judgment) insulting. A parallel to this is the arrogant presumption on the part of heterosexual people that anyone they meet is heterosexual. The question often must be *made* to arise, blatantly and explicitly, before the heterosexual person will consider the thought that one is lesbian or homosexual. Otherwise, even if some doubt arises, one will be given the dubious benefit of the doubt rather than be thought "ill" of, that is, suspected of "deviance."

The parallelism of heterosexuality and whiteness holds up in at least one more respect. In both cases there are certain members of the dominant group who systematically do *not* give the benefit of *their* doubt. They seem on the lookout for people whom they can suppose want to pass as members of their club. These are the sorts of people who are fabulously sensitive to clues that someone is Mulatto, Jewish, Indian or gay, and are eager to notify others of the person's supposed pretense of being "normal" or "white" (or whatever), though the person may have been making no pretense at all.* This latter type is quite commonly recognized as a racist, anti-Semite or homophobe, while the other type, the one who "graciously" lets the possibly deviant/dark person pass as normal/white, is often considered a nice person and not a bigot. People of both types seem to me to be equally arrogant: both

---

* I have not generally included Jews in my lists of examples of "racial" groups because when I did, Jewish critics of this material said that the ways in which anti-Semitism and other sorts of racism are similar and different make such simple inclusion misleading. I include Jews among my examples right here because with respect specifically to these questions of being allowed or not allowed to "pass" (whether one wants to or not), anti-Semitism and other kinds of racism are similar. Although many Jews are politically white in many ways in this country, when they "pass" as non-Jewish, what they may get is the treatment and reception accorded to ordinary "white" Americans. Paradoxically, though Jewish is not equivalent to nonwhite, passing still seems to be passing as white. My thanks to Nancy Bereano for useful discussion of these matters.

are arrogating definitional power to themselves and thereby asserting that defining is exclusively their prerogative.

I think that almost all white people engage in the activity of defining membership in the group of white people in one or another of these modes, quite un-self-consciously and quite constantly. It is very hard, in individual cases, to give up this habit and await people's deciding for themselves what group they are members of.

The tendency of members of the group called white to be generously inclusive, to count as white anybody not obviously nonwhite, seems to be of a piece with another habit of members of that group, namely, the habit of false universalization. As feminists we are very familiar with the male version of this: the men write and speak and presumably, therefore, also think, as though whatever is true of them is true of everybody. White people also speak in universals. A great deal of what has been written by white feminists is limited by this sort of false universalization. Much of what we have said is accurate only if taken to be about white women and white men within white culture (middle-class white women and white men, in fact). For the most part, it never occurred to us to modify our nouns accordingly; to our minds the people we were writing about were *people*. We don't think of ourselves as *white*.

It is an important breakthrough for a member of a dominant group to come to know s/he is a member of *a group,* to know that what s/he is is only *a part* of humanity. It was breathtaking to discover that in the culture I was born and reared in, the word 'woman' means *white woman,* just as we discovered before that the word 'man' means *male man.* This sudden expansion of the scope of one's perception can produce a cold rush of awareness of the arbitrariness of the definitions, the brittleness of these boundaries. Escape becomes thinkable.

The group to which I belong, presumably by virtue of my pigmentation, is not ordained in Nature to be socially and politically recognized as *a group,* but is so ordained only by its own members through their own self-serving and politically motivated hoarding of definitional power. What this can mean to white people is that we are not white by nature but by political classification, and hence it is in principle possible to disaffiliate. If being white is not finally a matter of skin color, which is beyond our power to change, but of politics and power, then perhaps white individuals in a white supremacist society are not doomed to dominance by logic or nature.

III

Some of my experience has made me feel trapped and set up so that my actions are caught in a web that connects them inexorably to sources in white privilege and to consequences oppressive to people of color (especially to women of color). Clearly, if one wants to extricate oneself from such a fate or (if the feeling was deceptive) from such a feeling of fatedness, the first rule for the procedure can only be: educate oneself.

One can, and should, educate oneself and overcome the terrible limitations imposed by the abysmal ignorance inherent in racism. There are traps, of course. For instance, one may slip into a frame of mind which distances those one is learning about as "objects of study." While one is educating oneself about the experiences and perspectives of the peoples one is ignorant about, and in part as a corrective to the errors of one's ways, one should also be studying one's own ignorance. Ignorance is not something simple: it is not a simple lack, absence or emptiness, and it is not a passive state. Ignorance of this sort—the determined ignorance most white Americans have of American Indian tribes and clans, the ostrichlike ignorance most white Americans have of the histories of Asian peoples in this country, the impoverishing ignorance most white Americans have of Black language—ignorance of these sorts is a complex result of many acts and many negligences.

To begin to appreciate this one need only hear the active verb
'to ignore' in the word 'ignorance'. Our ignorance is perpetu-
ated for us in many ways and we have many ways of perpetu-
ating it for ourselves.

I was at a poetry reading by the Black lesbian feminist,
Audre Lorde. In her poems she invoked African goddesses,
naming several of them. After the reading a white woman
rose to speak. She said first that she was very ignorant of
African religious and cultural history, and then she asked the
poet to spell the names of these goddesses and to tell her
where she might look for their stories. The poet replied by
telling her that there is a bibliography in the back of the book
from which she was reading which would provide the relevant
information. The white woman did not thank the poet and
sit down. The white woman (who I know is literate) said, "I
see, but will you spell their names for me?" What I saw was a
white woman committed to her ignorance and being stubborn
in its defense. She would convince herself that she cannot use
this bibliography if the Black woman will not spell the names
for her. She will say she tried to repair her ignorance but the
poet would not cooperate. The poet. The Black woman poet
who troubled herself to include a bibliography in her book of
poems.*

In Ralph Ellison's *The Invisible Man*[3] (a book of considerable value to feminists), one can see the structures of white
*ignora*nce from the side of the ignored. Nothing the protag-
onist can do makes him visible. He wants nothing so badly
as to be seen and heard. But he is frustrated by an opaque
and dense veil made up of lies the white men tell each other
about Black men. He is ignored nearly to death.

There is an enlightening account of some structures of
white ignorance also in a story called "Meditations on His-

---

* I do not mean to suggest she provided the bibliography specifically or
primarily for the education of white women; but it is reasonable to
assume she thought it would be useful to whatever white woman might
happen along with suitable curiosity.

tory," by Sherley Ann Williams.[4]   In the story, a man who is writing a book about how to manage slaves is visiting a place where a slave woman is being held until her baby is born so that, when they hang her for running away and killing a white man, her owner will at least have the baby to make up for his loss. The writer is interviewing the woman to find out why she killed the slave trader, and why and how the slaves got loose. (His ignorance is, of course, already showing, along with some of the structures which both motivate and support it.) He is irritated by her humming and singing, but it never occurs to him that it means anything. By way of her songs, the woman is able to conspire with the other slaves around the place; she tells them that her friends will come to rescue her and notifies them when the time is at hand; they cooperate with her, and she escapes. The hapless interviewer is totally baffled by her escape. His presumptions have closed out knowledge; his ignorance has been self-constructed. His ignorance has also been both encouraged and used by the slave woman, who has deliberately and reasonably played on it by pretending to be stupid, robotic and disoriented. It was certainly not in her interest to disabuse him of his assumptions that her singing was mindless and that she was too mindless to be plotting an escape. Ignorance works like this, creating the conditions which ensure its continuance.

White women can dip into our own experience as women for knowledge of the ways in which ignorance is complex and willful, for we know from our interactions with white men (and not necessarily only with men who are white) the "absence" imposed on us by our not being taken seriously, and we sense its motivation and know it is not simply accidental oversight.

If one wonders at the mechanisms of ignorance, at how a person can be right there and see and hear, and yet not know, one of the answers lies with the matter of attention. The man in Williams' story constantly daydreams about what a great success his book is going to be; he has compelling fantasies of his own fame and recognition—recognition by white men, of course. He is much more intent upon the matter of whom he will please and impress than he is upon the matter at hand. Members of dominant groups are habitually busy with impressing each other and care more for that than for actually knowing what is going on. And again, white women can learn from our own experience *a propos* (most often, white) men. We do much of what we do with a great anxiety for how we will be received by men—by mentors, friends, husbands, lovers, editors, members of our disciplines, professions or political groups, tenure-review committees, fathers. With our attention focused on these men, or our imaginings of them, we cannot pay attention to the matter at hand and will wind up ignorant of things which were perfectly apparent. Thus, without any specific effort these men can turn white women to the work of falsification even as we try to educate ourselves. Since white women are *almost* white men, being white, at least, and sometimes more-or-less honorary men, we can cling to a hope of true membership in the dominant and powerful group, and if our focus is thus locked on them by this futile hope, we can be stuck in our ignorance and theirs all our lives. (Some men of color fall into the parallel trap of hoping for membership in the dominant and powerful group, this time because of their sex. With their attention focused on power and money, they cannot see women, of their race or any other.) Attention has everything to do with knowledge.

IV

White women's attachments to white men have a great deal to do with our race privilege, with our racism and with our inabilities to understand these. Race and racism also have a great deal to do with white women's attachment to white men. We need to look at these connections more closely.

Within the span of a few days, a little while back, I encountered three things that came together like pieces of a simple
puzzle:

1. I heard a report on the radio about the "new" Klan. It included a recording of a man making a speech to the effect
that the white race is threatened with extinction. He explicitly compared the white race to the species of animals
that are classed as "endangered" and protected by laws.
He also noted with concern the fact that ten years ago the
population of Canada was 98 percent white and it is now
only 87 percent white.*

2. In a report in the feminist newspaper *Big Mama Rag,* it was
pointed out that "they" are making it virtually impossible
for white women to get abortions while forcing sterilization
of women of color both in the United States and around
the world.

3. In the feminist magazine *Conditions, No. 7,* there was a
conversation among several Black and Jewish lesbians.
Among other things, they discussed the matter of the pressure on them to have Black or Jewish babies, to contribute
to the survival of their races, which are threatened with extinction.**

I think on all this. For hundreds of years and for a variety
of reasons, mostly economic, white men of European stock
have been out, world-wide, conquering, colonizing and enslaving people they classify as dark, earning the latter's hatred
and rage in megadeath magnitudes. For hundreds of years,
those same white men have known they were a minority in

---

* This report went by quickly and I had no way to take notes, so I cannot vouch either for his statistics or for the absolute accuracy of my report of his statistics, but these figures do accurately reflect the general
magnitude of "the problem" and of *his* problem.

** Many Blacks in this country have a global perspective which reveals
that though white racism here has its genocidal aspect, Blacks in America are certainly not the whole Black race. For such people, the idea
that their race is threatened with extinction may not have the force it
would have for those with a more "american" perspective.

the population of the world, and more recently many of them
have believed in the doctrine that darkness is genetically dominant. White men have their reasons to be afraid of racial extinction.*

I begin to think that this fear is one of the crucial sources
of white racism even among the nonrabid who do not actively
participate in Klan Kulture. This suggests a reading of the
dominant culture's immense pressure on "women" to be
mothers. The dominant culture is white, and its pressure is
on white women to have white babies. The magazine images
of the glories of motherhood do not show white mothers with
little brown babies. Feminists have commonly recognized
that the pressures of compulsory motherhood on women of
color is not just pressure to keep women down but pressure
to keep the populations of their races up; we have not so
commonly thought that the pressures of compulsory motherhood on white women are not just pressures to keep women
down, but pressure to keep the white population up.

This aspect of compulsory motherhood for white women—
white men's anxiety for the survival of their race**—has not
been explicit or articulate in the lifetimes and lives of white
women in my circles, and the pressure to make babies has
been moderated by the pressure for "family planning" (which
I interpret as a project of quality control). But what *is* com-

---

* Male chauvinism makes the men think of themselves as the white
race. In this context it is appropriate to call it *their* race, not "our"
race.

** Edward Fields, a principal ideologue and propagandist for the Klan,
was asked if homosexuals are a threat to the white race. He replied that
they are, and went on to say: "Our birthrate is extremely low. We're
below population zero, below 2.5 children per family. The white race
is going down fast, we're only 12 percent of the world population. In
1990 we'll be only 10 percent of the population worldwide. We'll be
an extinct species if homosexuality continues to grow, interracial marriage continues to take people out of the white race, if our birthrate
continues to fall." (Quoted in "Into The Fires of Hatred: A Portrait
of Klan Leader Edward Fields," by Lee David Hoshall with Nancy A.F.
Langer, in *Gay Community News*, November 6, 1982, p. 5.)

mon and overt in primarily white circles where the racism
runs deep and mostly silent is another curious phenomenon.

In the all white or mostly white environments I have usually lived and worked in, when the women start talking up feminism and lesbian feminism, we are very commonly challenged
with the claim that if we had our way, the species would die
out. (The assumption our critics make here is that if women
had a choice, we would never have intercourse and never bear
children. This reveals a lot about the critics' own assessment
of the joys of sex, pregnancy, birthing and motherhood.)
They say the species would die out. What I suspect is that the
critics confuse the white race with the human species, just as
men have confused males with the human species. What the
critics are saying, once it is decoded, is that the white race
might die out. The demand that white women make white
babies to keep the race afloat has not been overt, but I think
it is being made over and over again in disguised form as a
preachment within an all-white context about our duty to
keep the species afloat.

Many white women, certainly many white feminists in the
milieux I am familiar with, have not consciously thought that
white men may be fearing racial extinction and, at the least,
wanting our services to maintain their numbers. Perhaps here
in middle America, most white women are so secure in white
dominance that such insecure thoughts as whether there are
enough white people around do not occur. But also, because
we white women have been able to think of ourselves as looking just at *women* and *men* when we really were looking at
white women and white men, we have generally interpreted
our connections with these men solely in terms of gender, sexism and male dominance. We have to figure their desire for
racial dominance into the equations.

Simply as females, as mere women in this world, we who
are female and white stand to be poor, ill-educated, preyed
upon and despised. But because we are both female *and white*,
we belong to that group of women from which the men of the
racially dominant group choose their mates. Because of that

we are given some access to the benefits they have as members
of the racially dominant male group—access to material and
educational benefits and the specious benefits of enjoying
secondhand feelings of superiority and supremacy. We also
have the specious benefit of a certain *hope* (a false hope, as it
turns out) which women of subordinated races do not have,
namely the hope of becoming actually dominant *with* the
white men, as their "equals." This last pseudo-benefit binds
us most closely to them in racial solidarity. A liberal white
feminism would seek "equality"; we can hardly expect to be
heard as saying we want social and economic status equal to
that of, say, Chicanos. If what we want is equality with our
white brothers, then what we want is, among other things, our
own firsthand participation in racial dominance rather than
the secondhand ersatz dominance we get as the dominant
group's women. No wonder such feminism has no credibility
with women of color.

Race is a tie that binds us to men: "us" being white wom-
en, and "men" being white men. If we wish not to be bound
in subordination to men, we have to give up trading on our
white skin for white men's race privilege. And on the other
hand, if we detach ourselves from reproductive service to
white men (in the many senses and dimensions of "reproduction"), the threat we pose is not just to their male selves but
to their white selves. White men's domination and control of
white women is essential to their project of maintaining their
racial dominance. This is probably part of the explanation of
why the backlash against feminism overlaps in time and per-
sonnel with renewed intensity and overtness of white racism
in this country. When their control of "their" women is
threatened, their confidence in their racial dominance is
threatened.

It is perfectly clear that this did not occur to many of us in
advance, but for white women a radical feminism is treacher-
ous to the white race as presently constructed and instituted
in this country. The growing willingness of white women to
forego the material benefits and ego supports available

through connections with white men makes us much harder
to contain and control as part of the base of their racial dominance. For many of us, resistance to white male domination
was first, and quite naturally, action simply for our own re-
lease from a degradation and tyranny we hated in and of itself.
But in this racial context, our pursuit of our liberation (I do
not say "of equality") is, whether or not we so intend it, disloyal to Whiteness.

I recommend that we make this disloyalty an explicit part
of our politics and embrace it, publicly. This can help us to
steer clear of a superficial politics of just wanting what our
white brothers have, and help us develop toward a genuine
disaffiliation from that Whiteness that has, finally, so little to
do with skin color and so much to do with racism.

V

In a certain way it is true that being white-skinned means
that everything I do will be wrong—at the least an exercise of
unwarranted privilege—and I will encounter the reasonable
anger of women of color at every turn. But 'white' also des-
ignates a political category, a sort of political fraternity.
Membership in it is not in the same sense "fated" or "natural." It can be resisted.

There is a correct line on the matter of white racism which
is, in fact, quite correct, to the effect that as a white person
one must never claim not to be racist, but only to be anti-
racist. The reasoning is that racism is so systematic and white
privilege so impossible to escape, that one is, simply, trapped.
On one level this is perfectly true and must always be taken
into account. Taken as the whole and final truth, it is also
unbearably and dangerously dismal. It would place us in the
hopeless moral position of one who believes in original sin
but in no mechanism of redemption. But white supremacy is
not a law of nature, nor is any individual's complicity in it.

Feminists make use of a distinction between being male and being "a man," or masculine. I have enjoined males of my acquaintance to set themselves against masculinity. I have asked them to think about how they can stop being men, and I was not recommending a sex-change operation. I do not know how they can stop being men, but I think it is thinkable, and it is a counsel of hope. Likewise I can set myself against Whiteness: I can give myself the injunction to stop being White.

I do not suggest for a moment that I can disaffiliate by a private act of will, or by any personal strategy. Nor, certainly, is it accomplished simply by thinking it possible. To think it thinkable shortcuts no work and shields one from no responsibility. Quite the contrary, it may be a necessary prerequisite to assuming responsibility, and it invites the honorable work of radical imagination.

NOTES

1. Persephone Press, Watertown, Massachusetts, 1980.

2. Cf., "The Problem That Has No Name," in this collection, for discussion of the speciousness and of the effectiveness of such power.

3. Random House, New York, 1952.

4. In *Midnight Birds, Stories of Contemporary Black Women Writers,* edited by Mary Helen Washington (Anchor Doubleday, New York, 1980).

LESBIAN FEMINISM AND THE GAY RIGHTS MOVEMENT: ANOTHER VIEW OF MALE SUPREMACY, ANOTHER SEPARATISM*

Many gay men and some lesbians and feminists assume that it is reasonable to expect lesbian and feminist support for, or participation in, gay political and cultural organizations and projects, and many people think it is reasonable to expect that gay men will understand and support feminist and lesbian causes. But both of these expectations are, in general, conspicuously not satisfied.

With a few exceptions, lesbians—and in particular, feminist lesbians—have not seen gay rights as a compelling cause nor found association with gay organizations rewarding enough to hold more than temporary interest. With perhaps even fewer

---

* This essay is a revision of a talk I gave at an event in the Spring of 1981, in Grand Rapids, Michigan, organized by the Grand Rapids chapter of the gay catholic organization, Dignity, and co-sponsored by Aradia. My thanks to Larry Manglitz and Calien Lewis for seeing the need, and doing something about it.

exceptions, gay men do not find feminist or lesbian concerns to be close enough to their own to compel either supportive political action or serious and attentive thought. Gay political and cultural organizations which ostensibly welcome and act in behalf of both gay men and gay women generally have few if any lesbian members, and lesbian and feminist political and cultural organizations, whether or not they seek or accept male membership, have little if any gay male support.

All of us deviants suffer from the fact that the dominant culture is, at least publicly, intolerant of deviations from what might be called "missionary sexuality": sexuality organized around male-dominant, female-subordinate genital intercourse. Lesbians and gay men both are subject to derision and ostracism, abuse and terror, in both cases for reasons that flow somehow out of social and political structures of sex and gender. Popular images of the lesbian and the gay man are images of people who do not fit the patterns of gender imposed on the sexes. She is seen as a female who is not feminine and he as a male who is not masculine. In many states and locales lesbians and gay men find themselves joined under a common political necessity when they must battle a Proposition This-or-That which would legally sanction their civil injury, or are under assault by such groups as the Moral Majority or the Ku Klux Klan. Gay men seem to many women to be less sexist than straight men, presumably because gay men are not interested in women sexually. And the feminist commitment to individual sexual self-determination includes, for most feminists, a commitment to gay rights.

Such things might lead one to suppose that there is, in fact, a cultural and political affinity between gay men on the one hand and women—lesbians and/or feminists—on the other, and then to assume that the absence of any firm and general alliance here must be explained by there being some sort of hitch or barrier, some accidental factor of style, language or misinformation, which obscures the common interests or makes cooperation difficult. I do not share this supposition and assumption.

A culture hostile to any but missionary sexuality is also hostile to women—the culture is a sexist, a misogynist, a male-supremacist culture. Because of this cultural reality, the worlds of what the clinicians would call "homosexual" women and men are very different: we deviate from very different norms; our deviations are situated very differently in the male-supremacist world view and political structure; we are not objects of the same phobias and loathings. If some of us feel some threads of sympathy connecting us and therefore would want to be friends to each other's causes, the first thing we should do is seek a just understanding of the differences which separate us. But these differences turn out to be so profound as to cast doubt on the assumption that there is any basic cultural or political affinity here at all upon which alliances could be built.

A look at some of the principles and values of male-supremacist society and culture suggests immediately that the male gay rights movement and gay male culture, as they can be known in their public manifestations, are in many central points considerably more congruent than discrepant with this phallocracy, which in turn is so hostile to women and to the woman-loving to which lesbians are committed. Among the most fundamental of those principles and values are the following:

1. The presumption of male citizenship.
2. Worship of the penis.
3. Male homoeroticism, or man-loving.
4. Contempt for women, or woman-hating.
5. Compulsory male heterosexuality.
6. The presumption of general phallic access.

As one explores the meaning of these principles and values, gay and straight male cultures begin to look so alike that it becomes something of a puzzle why straight men do not recognize their gay brothers, as they certainly do not, much to the physical and psychological expense of the latter.

1. The presumption of male citizenship is the principle that if, and only if, someone is male, he has a *prima facie* claim to a certain array of rights, such as the rights to ownership and disposition of property, to physical integrity and freedom of movement, to having a wife and to paternity, to access to resources for making a living, and so forth.* Though dominant men accept among themselves certain sorts of justifications for abridging or denying such rights of men (e.g., the necessity of raising an army), the presumption is on the side of their having these rights. If others deny a man these rights arbitrarily, that is, apparently without recognizing that such denial requires certain sorts of justification, then the implication arises that he is not really or fully a man or male. If he accepts the burden of proof, this too would suggest that he is not really or fully a man or male. Thus, what is called "discrimination"—the arbitrary abridgment of men's rights, abridgement not accompanied by certain sorts of justification —is felt as "emasculating," and those whose rights are abridged are inclined to respond by asserting their manhood.

Civil rights movements of various sorts in this country, under male leadership, have tended to take this approach which obviously does not question, but relies on, the underlying presumption of male citizenship. A civil-rights feminism, even one which means to be moderate, is pushed toward challenging this presumption, hence toward a more radical challenge to the prevailing order, by the fact that its constituency is women.** Women's only alternative to the more radical challenge is that of claiming the manhood of women,

---

* Obviously, what is considered a right of citizenship varies from nation to nation, and within nations men have among themselves more than one class of citizenship.

** There are good political reasons why it took 72 years from the first public demand for woman suffrage to the ratification of the suffrage amendment, and why the Equal Rights Amendment, which was first taken up by Congress in 1920 has not yet, 64 years later, become law. The principle of male (and not female) citizenship is very basic to phallocratic society.

which has been tried and is not in my estimation as absurd at as it may sound; but that claim is not easy to explain or to incorporate in persuasive political rhetoric.

Since the constituency of the male gay rights movement is very overtly and definitively classified and degraded as "womanish" or "effeminate," it might seem that a logical and proud gay political strategy would be to demand citizenship as "women"—the strategy of challenging the presumption of male citizenship. Some individual gay men lean toward this, and thus to political kinship with women, but the gay rights movement generally has taken the course of claiming the manhood of its constituents, supposing that the presumption of gay men's rights will follow upon acknowledgement of this. In so doing, they acquiesce in and support the reservation of full citizenship to males and thus align themselves with the political adversaries of feminism.

It is indeed true that gay men, generally speaking, are really men and thus by the logic of phallocratic thinking really ought to be included under the presumption of male citizenship. In fact, as some gay men have understood (even if the popular mind has not), gay men generally are in significant ways, perhaps in all important ways, only more loyal to masculinity and male-supremacy than other men.*

2. In phallocratic culture, the penis is deified, fetishized, mystified and worshipped. Male literature proves with convincing redundancy that straight men identify with their penises and are simultaneously strangely alienated from them.** The culture is one in which men are not commonly found laughable when they characterize the female as a castrated male. It is a culture in which an identification of the penis

---

* The homoeroticism celebrated in Plato's *Symposium* and applauded in some contemporary gay circles is clearly both generally elitist and specifically male-supremacist.

** As C. Shafer pointed out to me, according to this use of "identify with," the identification presupposes the alienation since one can only identify with something that is other than oneself.

with power, presence and creativity is found plausible—not the brain, the eyes, the mouth or the hand, but the penis. In that culture, any object or image which at all resembles or suggests the proportions of an erect penis will be imbued with or assumed to have special mythic, semantic, psychological or supernatural powers. There is nothing in gay male culture or politics as they appear on the street, in bars, in gay media, which challenges this belief in the magic of the penis. In the straight culture, worship of the penis in symbolic representations is overt and common, but men's love of penises in the flesh tends to be something of a closet affair, expressed privately or covertly, or disguised by humor or rough housing. Gay men generally are only much more straightforward about it: less ambivalent, less restrained, more overt.

If worship of the phallus is central to phallocratic culture, then gay men, by and large, are more like ardent priests than infidels, and the gay rights movement may be the fundamentalism of the global religion which is Patriarchy. In this matter, the congruence of gay male culture with straight male culture and the chasm between these and women's cultures are great indeed.

Women generally have good experiential reason to associate negative values and feelings with penises, since penises are connected to a great extent with their degradation, terror and pain. The fear or dread this can generate might be a close relative of worship, but there is also the not-so-uncommon experience of boredom, frustration and alienation in the sorts of encounters with penises which are advertised as offering excitement, fulfillment and transcendence. So far as living with the threat of rape permits, many women's attitudes toward penises tend to vacillate between indifference and contempt, attitudes which are contraries of worship. Lesbians and feminists, who may know more securely the dispensibility of penises to women's physical gratification and to their identity and authority, may be even more prone than most women to these unworshipful attitudes. It is among women, especially feminists and lesbians, that the unbelievers are to be found.

We and gay men are on opposite sides of this part of phallo-philic orthodoxy.

Let me interject that though I derogate and mock the worship of the penis, I do not despise its enjoyment. I suspect that if penises were enjoyed a good deal more and worshipped a great deal less, everyone's understanding of both male and female sexuality, of power and of love, would change beyond recognition and much for the better. But I do not read gay male culture as that radical a culture of enjoyment, in spite of its hedonistic rhetoric and the number of good cooks it produces. There are suggestions of this heresy at its outer margins only, and I will return to that matter later.

3. The third principle of male-supremacy I listed above is the principle of male homoeroticism. I am not speaking of some sort of "repressed" homosexuality to which the intense heterosexuality of so many men is said to be a reaction. I speak here not of homosexuality but of homoeroticism, and I think it is not in the least repressed.

In the dominant straight male language and world view, "sex" equals what I have called "missionary sex." In spite of the variety of things people actually do with and to each other in private under the rubrics of "having sex" or "being sexual," cultural images of sex and "sexual acts" refer and pertain overwhelmingly to male-dominant, female-subordinate genital intercourse, that is, to fucking. As has often been documented, most men claim, indeed insist, that there is no essential connection between sex (that is, fucking) and love, affection, emotional connection, admiration, honor or any of the other passions of desire and attachment. To say that straight men are heterosexual is only to say that they engage in sex (fucking) exclusively with (or upon or to) the other sex, i.e., women.* All or almost all of that which pertains to

---

* When a man who considers himself firmly heterosexual fucks a boy or another man, generally he considers the other to be a woman or to be made a woman by this act.

love, most straight men reserve exclusively for other men. The people whom they admire, respect, adore, revere, honor, whom they imitate, idolize, and form profound attachments to, whom they are willing to teach and from whom they are willing to learn, and whose respect, admiration, recognition, honor, reverence and love they desire. . .those are, overwhelmingly, other men. In their relations with women, what passes for respect is kindness, generosity or paternalism; what passes for honor is removal to the pedestal. From women they want devotion, service and sex.

Heterosexual male culture is homoerotic; it is man-loving. This is perfectly consistent with its being hetero-sex-ual, since in this scheme sex and love have nothing essential, and very little that is accidental, to do with each other.

Gay male culture is also homoerotic. There is almost nothing of it which suggests any extension of love to women, and all of the elements of passion and attachment, including all kinds of sensual pleasure and desire, are overtly involved in its male-male relations. Man-loving is, if anything, simply more transparent to the lovers and more complete for gay men than for straight men.

Lesbian and lesbian-feminist culture is also, of course, generally homoerotic. Lesbians/feminists tend to reserve passion, attachment and desire for women, and to want them from women. We tend to be relatively indifferent, erotically, to men, so far as socialization and survival in male-supremacist culture permit. Not to love men is, in male-supremacist culture, possibly the single most execrable sin. It is indicative of this, I think, that lesbians' or feminists' indifference to men is identified directly as man-hating. Not to love men is so vile in this scheme of values that it cannot be conceived as the merely negative thing it is, as a simple absence of interest, but must be seen as positive enmity.

If man-loving is the rule of phallocratic culture, as I think it is, and if, therefore, male homoeroticism is compulsory, then gay men should be numbered among the faithful, or the loyal and law-abiding citizens, and lesbians feminists are sinners and criminals, or, if perceived politically, insurgents and traitors.

4. Given the sharpness of the male/female and masculine/ feminine dualism of phallocratic thought, woman-hating is an obvious corollary of man-loving.

Contempt for women is such a common thing in this culture that it is sometimes hard to see. It is expressed in a great deal of what passes for humor, and in most popular entertainment. Its presence also in high culture and scholarship has been documented exhaustively by feminist scholars in every field. It is promoted by the advertising and fashion industries. All heterosexual pornography, including man-made so-called "lesbian" pornography for male audiences, exhibits absolutely uncompromising woman-hating.[1] Athletics coaches and military drill sergeants express their disgust when their charges perform inadequately by calling them "women," "ladies," "girls" and other more derogatory names for females.

Woman-hating is a major part of what supports male-supremacy; its functions in phallocratic society are many. Among other things, it supports male solidarity by setting women both apart from and below men. It helps to maintain a clear and definitive boundary between the male "us" and its corresponding "them," and it helps to sustain the illusion of superiority which motivates loyalty. Men not uncommonly act out contempt for women ritually to express and thereby reconfirm for themselves and each other their manhood, that is, their loyal partisanship of the male "us" and their rights to the privileges of membership. This is one of the functions of the exchanges of "conquest" stories, of casual derogation, gang rape, and other such small and large atrocities.[2]

In a woman-hating culture, one of the very nasty things that can happen to a man is his being treated or seen as a woman, or womanlike. This degradation makes him a proper object of rape and derision, and reverses for him the presumption of civil rights. This dreadful fate befalls gay men. In the

society at large, if it is known that a man is gay, he is subject
to being pegged at the level of sexual status, personal authority and civil rights which are presumptive for women. This is,
of course, really quite unfair, for most gay men are quite as
fully *men* as any men: being gay is not at all inconsistent
with being loyal to masculinity and committed to contempt
for women. Some of the very things which lead straight people to doubt gay men's manhood are, in fact, proofs of it.

One of the things which persuades the straight world that
gay men are not really men is the effeminacy of style of some
gay men and the gay institution of the impersonation of wom-
en, both of which are associated in the popular mind with
male homosexuality. But as I read it, gay men's effeminacy
and donning of feminine apparel displays no love of or identification with women or the womanly.

For the most part, this femininity is affected and is characterized by theatrical exaggeration. It is a casual and cynical
mockery of women, for whom femininity is the trappings of
oppression, but it is also a kind of play, a toying with that
which is taboo. It is a naughtiness indulged in, I suspect,
more by those who believe in their immunity to contamina-
tion than by those with any doubts or fears. Cocky lads who
are sure of their immortality are the ones who do acrobatics
on the ledge five stories above the pavement. What gay male
affectation of femininity seems to me to be is a kind of serious sport in which men may exercise their power and control
over the feminine, much as in other sports one exercises physical power and control over elements of the physical universe.
Some gay men achieve, indeed, prodigious mastery of the feminine, and they are often treated by those in the know with
the respect due to heroes.* But the mastery of the feminine
is not feminine. It is masculine. It is not a manifestation of

---

* Female-impersonators are a staple in the entertainment provided at
gay bars and clubs, and they play to a very appreciative audience. Their
skill is recognized and admired. The best of them travel around, like
other entertainers, and their stage names are well known all over the
country. They are idols of a sort.

woman-loving but of woman-hating. Someone with such mastery may have the very first claim to manhood.

All this suggests that there is more than a little truth in the common claim that homophobia belongs most to those least secure in their masculinity. Blatant and flagrant gay male effeminacy ridicules straight men's anxious and superstitious avoidance of the feminine.[3] And there are gay men who are inclined to cheer this account, to feel smug and delighted at an analysis like this which suggests that they are superior to other men, that is, superior in their masculinity. They clearly reveal thereby that they do indeed pass the Contempt-for-Women test of manhood.[4]

(There is a gentler politic which lies behind some gay men's affectation of the feminine. It can be a kind of fun which involves mockery not of women or of straight men but of the whole institution of gender—a deliberately irreverent fooling around with one of the most sacred foolishnesses of phallo-cratic culture. This may be the necessarily lighthearted political action of a gender rebel rather than an exercise of masculinity. Certain kinds of lightheartedness in connection with what is, after all, the paraphernalia of women's oppression can become a rather bad joke. But when the silliness stays put as a good joke on patriarchy it betrays a potentially revolutionary levity about the serious matter of manhood and thus may express a politics more congenial to feminism than most gay politics.)

One might have hoped that since gay men themselves can be, in a way, victims of woman-hating, they might have come to an unusual identification with women and hence to political alliance with them. This is a political possibility which is in some degree actualized by some gay men, but for most, such identification is really impossible. They know, even if not articulately, that their classification with women is based on a profound misunderstanding. Like most other men who for one reason or another get a taste of what it's like to be a woman in a woman-hating culture, they are inclined to protest, not the injustice of anyone ever being treated so shabbily, but the injustice of *their* being treated so when *they* are not women. The straight culture's identification of gay men with women usually only serves to intensify gay men's investment in their difference and distinction from the female other. What results is not alliance with women but strategies designed to demonstrate publicly gay men's identification with men, as over and against women. Such strategies must involve one form or another of public acting out of male-dominance and female-subordination.

It is not easy to find ways to stage public actions and appearances which present simultaneously the gayness of gay men and their correct male-supremacist contempt for women. Affected effeminacy does display this, but it is popularly misunderstood. It would be perfect if some of the many gay men who are married would appear with their wives on talk shows where the men would talk animatedly about the joys of loving men and their wives would smile and be suitably supportive, saying they only want their husbands to be happy. But there will not be many volunteers for this work. Who then are the women who will appear slightly to the side of and slightly behind gay men, representing the female other in the proper relation and contrast to their manhood? Lesbians, of course. Gay men can credibly present themselves as men, that is, as beings defined by superiority to women, if there are lesbians in the gay rights movement—given only that males are always or almost always in the visible position of leadership. By having females around, visible but in subordinate positions, gay men can publicly demonstrate their separation and distinction from women and their "appropriate" attitude toward women, which is, at bottom, woman-hating.[5]

Gay male culture and the male gay rights movement, in their publicly visible manifestations, seem to conform quite nicely to the fundamental male-supremacist principle of woman-hating. Anyone who has hung around a gay bar would expect as much: gay men, like other men, commonly, casually and cheerfully make jokes which denigrate and vilify women, women's bodies, women's genitals.[6] Indeed, in some circles,

contempt for women and physical disgust with female bodies
are overtly accepted as just the other side of the coin of gay
men's attraction to men.

5. The fifth of the principles of male-supremacy which I
listed was the principle of compulsory heterosexuality. It is
a rule about having sex, that is, about "missionary" fucking.
This activity is generally compulsory for males in this culture.
Fucking is a large part of how females are kept subordinated
to males. It is a ritual enactment of that subordination which
constantly reaffirms the fact of subordination and habituates
both men and women to it, both in body and in imagination.
It is also one of the components of the system of behavior
and values which constitutes compulsory motherhood for
women. A great deal of fucking is also presumed to preserve
and maintain women's belief in their own essential heterosexuality, which in turn (for women as not for men) connects
with and reinforces female hetero-eroticism, that is, man-
loving in women. It is very important to the maintenance of
male-supremacy that men fuck women, a lot. So it is required; it is compulsory. Doing it is both doing one's duty
and an expression of solidarity. A man who does not or will
not fuck women is not pulling his share of the load. He is not
a loyal and dependable member of the team.

Some gay men certainly are deviants in this respect, and
would lobby for tolerance of their deviance without the penalties now attached to it. They would break a rule of phallocracy, but in many cases they are loathe to do their duty
only because they have learned all too well their lessons in
woman-hating. Their reluctance to play out this part of manhood is due only to an imbalance, where the requisite woman-
hating has taken a form and reached an intensity which puts
it in tension with this other requirement of manhood. Such
divergence of gay life from male-supremacist culture clearly is
not a turning from fundamental male-supremacist values, so
much as it is a manifestation of the tensions internal to those
values.

The unwillingness of some gay men to engage in fucking women seems not to be central to male homosexuality, to "gayness," as it is presented and defended by the male gay rights movement. The latter seems for the most part tolerant of the requirement of heterosexuality; its spokesmen seem to demand merely that men not be limited to heterosexuality, that is, that genital contact and intercourse be permitted as part of their homoerotic relations with other men. They point out that a great many gay men are married, and that many men who engage in what is called homosexuality also do fuck women—that is, they are "normal" and dutiful men. They point out how many gay men are fathers. I do not pretend to know the demographics here: how many gay men do fuck women or have impregnated women, nor even how many are committed to this line of persuasion in their roles as gay rights activists. But this *is* one of the themes in gay rights rhetoric. Men who take such a line are, again, no particular political allies of women. They maintain their solidarity with other men in respect of this aspect of keeping the system going, and only want credit for it in spite of some of their other activities and proclivities.

6. We now come to the only one of the fundamental principles of male-supremacist culture and society where there really is an interesting divergence between it and the values and principles of what it labels male homosexuality. Even here, the situation is ambiguous, for the male gay rights movement only wants too much of something that is really already very dear to straight men.

Men in general in this culture consider themselves, in virtue of their genital maleness, to have a right to access to whatever they want. The kinds of limitations they recognize to this general accessibility of the universe to them are limitations imposed by other men through such things as systems of private property, the existence of the state, and the rules and rituals of limitations of violence among men. In their identification with Mankind, they recognize no limitations whatsoever on their access to anything else in the universe, with the possible exception of those imposed by the physical requirements of Mankind's own survival, and they may even ignore or scoff at those out of some strange belief in Mankind as immortal and eternal. The translation of this cosmic male arrogance to the level of the individual male body is the individual's presumption of the almost universal right to fuck—to assert his individual male dominance over all that is not himself by using it for his phallic gratification or self-assertion at either a physical or a symbolic level. Any physical object can be urinated on or in, or ejaculated on or in, or penetrated by his penis, as can any nonhuman animal or any woman, subject only to limitations imposed by property rights and local social mores—and even those are far from inviolable by the erect penis which, they say, has no conscience. The one general and nearly inviolable limitation on male phallic access is that males are not supposed to fuck other males, especially adult human males of their own class, tribe, race, etc. This is the one important rule of phallocratic culture that most gay men do violate, and this violation is central to what is defended and promoted by the male gay rights movement.

But note the form of this deviation from the rules of the male-supremacist game. It is refusing a limitation on phallic access; it is a refusal to restrain the male self. It is an excess of phallic arrogance. The fundamental principle is that of universal phallic access. What is in dispute is only a qualification of it. Gay male culture does not deny or shun the principle; it embraces it.

A large part of what maintains male-supremacy is the constant cultivation of masculinity in genital males. Masculinity involves the belief that, as a man, one is the center of a universe which is designed to feed and sustain one and to be ruled by one, as well as the belief that anything which does not conform to one's will may be, perhaps *should* be, brought into line by violence. Thus far, there really would not be room in the universe for more than one masculine being. There must be a balancing factor, something to protect the

masculine beings from each other. Sure enough, there is a
sort of "incest taboo" built in to standard masculinity: a
properly masculine being does not prey upon or consume other masculine beings in his kin group.* It is a moderating
theme like the rule of honor among thieves.

Within the kin group, masculine beings may compete in
various well-defined and ritualistic ways, but they identify
with each other in such a way that they cannot see each other
as the "Other," that is, as raw material for the gratification of
the appetites. This blending into a herd with certain other
masculine beings, which they sometimes call "male bonding,"
is what would guarantee masculine beings some crucial bit of
security among masculine beings who in infantile solipsistic
arrogance would otherwise blindly annihilate each other. The
proscription against male-male fucking is the lid on masculinity, the limiting principle which keeps masculinity from being
simply an endless firestorm of undifferentiated self. As such,
that proscription is necessarily always in tension with the rest
of masculinity. This tension gives masculinity its structure,
but it is also forever problematic. As long as males are social-
ized constantly to masculinity, the spectre of their running
amok is always present. The straight male's phobic reaction
to male homosexuality can then be seen as a fear of an unre-
stricted, unlimited, un*governed* masculinity. It is, of course,
more than this and more complicated; but is this, among
other things.

To assuage this fear, what the rhetoric and ideology of the
male gay rights movement has tried to do is to convince
straight men that male-male ass-fucking and fellatio are not
after all a violation of the rule against men preying upon or
consuming other men, but are, on the contrary, expressions
of male bonding. I do not pretend to know whether, or how

---

* I use the term "kin" here in a special sense. The group in question
may be defined more or less broadly by class, race, age, religious affil-
iation, ethnic origin, language, etc., and may be a street gang, a Mafia
"family," a corporation, students at a particular school, a political
machine, etc.

often, male-male ass-fucking or fellatio is basically rape or basically bonding, or how basically it is either, so I will not offer to settle that question. What I want to note is just this: if it is the claim of gay men and their movement that male-male fucking is really a form of male bonding, an intensification and completion of the male homoeroticism which is basic to male-supremacy, then they themselves are arguing that their culture and practices are, after all, perfectly congruent with the culture, practices and principles of male-supremacy.

According to the general picture that has emerged here, male homosexuality is congruent with and a logical extension of straight male-supremacist culture. It seems that straight men just don't understand the congruency and are frightened by the "logical extension." In response, the male gay rights movement attempts to educate and encourage straight men to an appreciation of the normalcy and harmlessness of gay men. It does not challenge the principles of male-supremacist culture.

In contrast, any politics which concerns itself with the dignity and welfare of women cannot fail to challenge these principles, and lesbian feminism in particular is totally at odds with them. The feminist lesbian's style, activities, desire and values are obviously and profoundly noncongruent with the principles of male-supremacist culture. She does not love men; she does not preserve all passion and significant exchange for men. She does not hate women. She presupposes the equality of the female and male bodies, or even the superiority or normativeness of the female body. She has no interest in penises beyond some reasonable concern about how men use them against women. She claims civil rights for women without arguing that women are really men with different plumbing. She does not live as the complement to the rule of heterosexuality for men. She is not accessible to the penis; she does not view herself as a natural object of fucking and denies that men have either the right or the duty to fuck her.

Our existence as females not owned by males and not penis-accessible, our values and our attention, our experience of the erotic and the direction of our passion, places us directly in opposition to male-supremacist culture in all respects, so much so that our existence is almost unthinkable within the world view of that culture.[7]

Far from there being a natural affinity between feminist lesbians and the gay civil rights movement, I see their politics as being, in most respects, directly antithetical to each other. The general direction of gay male politics is to claim maleness and male privilege for gay men and to promote the enlargement of the range of presumption of phallic access to the point where it is, in fact, absolutely unlimited. The general direction of lesbian feminist politics is the dismantling of male privilege, the erasure of masculinity, and the reversal of the rule of phallic access, replacing the rule that access is permitted unless specifically forbidden with the rule that it is forbidden unless specifically permitted.

There are other possibilities. Gay men, at least those who are not of the upper economic classes and/or are not white, do experience the hatred and fear and contempt of straight men,* do experience ostracism and abridgment of rights, or live with the threat thereof. Gay men are terrorized and victimized significantly more than other men of their class and race by the bullies, muggers and religious zealots of the world. They do tolerate, as do women, legal and nonlegal harassment and insult no self-respecting person should ever tolerate. Out of this marginalization and victimization there could and should come something more constructive, progressive—indeed revolutionary—than a politics of assimilation which con-

---

* And women, too, including some lesbians. But women's negative attitudes toward any group of men are not really as consequential as men's.

sists mainly of claims to manhood and pleas for understanding.

However a man comes to perceive himself as "different" with respect to his relation to the gender categories, in his sensual desires, in his passions, he comes so to perceive himself in a cultural context which offers him the duality masculine/feminine to box himself into. On the one hand, he is "offered" the dominant sexist and heterosexist culture which will label him feminine and castigate him, and on the other hand, he is "offered" a very misogynist and hypermasculine gay male subculture; he is invited to join a basically masculist gay rights movement mediating the two, trying to build bridges of understanding between them. If he has the aesthetic and political good taste to find all of the above repugnant, he can only do what lesbian feminists have been doing: *invent.* He has to move off, as we have, in previously indescribable directions. He has to invent what maleness is when it is not shaped and hardened into straight masculinity, gay hypermasculinity or effeminacy. For a man even to begin to think such invention is worthwhile or necessary is to be disloyal to phallocracy. For a gay man, it is to *be* the traitor to masculinity that the straight men always thought he was.

Any man who would be a friend to women must come to understand the values and principles of phallocratic culture and how his own life is interwoven with them, and must reject them and become disloyal to masculinity. Any man who would do this has to reinvent what being a man is. The initial intuition which many of us have had that gay men may be more prone than straight men to being friends to women has, perhaps, this much truth in it: for gay men, more than for straight men, the seeds both of some motive and of some resources for taking this radical turn are built into their cultural and political situation in the world. The gay man's difference can be the source of the friction which might mother invention and may provide resources for that invention.

One of the privileges of being normal and ordinary is a certain unconsciousness. When one is that which is taken as the norm in one's social environment, one does not have to think about it. Often, in discussions about prejudice and discrimination I hear statements like these: "I don't think of myself as heterosexual"; "I don't think of myself as white"; "I don't think of myself as a man"; "I'm just a person, I just think of myself as a person." If one is the norm, one does not have to know what one is.[8] If one is marginal, one does not have the privilege of not noticing what one is.

This absence of privilege is a presence of knowledge. As such, it can be a great resource, given only that the marginal person does not scorn the knowledge and lust for inclusion in the mainstream, for the unconsciousness of normalcy. I do not say this casually or callously; I know the longing for normalcy and the burden of knowledge. But the knowledge, and the marginality, can be embraced. The alternative to embracing them is erasing the meaning of one's own experience in order to blend in as normal—pretending that one's difference is nothing, really, nothing more significant than a preference for foreign cars, bourbon or western-cut clothes. Gay men and lesbians, all, are sexual deviants: our bodies move in this world on very different paths and encounter other bodies in very different ways and different places than do the bodies of the heterosexual majority. Nothing could be more fundamental. The difference is not "mere," not unimportant. Whatever there is in us that longs for integrity has to go with the knowledge, not with the desire to lose consciousness in normalcy.

I cannot tell another person how the knowledge of her or his marginality will ramify through lifelong experience to more knowledge, but I think it is safe to say that since our marginality has so centrally to do with our bodies and our bodies' nonconformance with the bodily and behavioral categories of the dominant cultures, we have access to knowledge of bodies which is lost and/or hidden in the dominant cultures. In particular, both gay men and lesbians may have access to knowledge of bodily, sensory, sensuous pleasure that is almost totally blocked out in heterosexual male-supremacist cultures, especially in the streams most dominated by white, christian, commercial and militaristic styles and values. To the extent that gay male culture cultivates and explores and expands its tendencies to the pursuit of simple bodily pleasure, as opposed to its tendencies to fetishism, fantasy and alienation, it seems that it could nurture very radical, hitherto unthinkable new conceptions of what it can be to live as a male body.

The phallocratic orthodoxy about the male body's pleasure seems to be that strenuous muscular exertion and the orgasm associated with fucking are its highest and greatest forms. This doctrine suits the purposes of a society which requires both intensive fucking and a population of males who imagine themselves as warriors. But what bodily pleasures there are in the acts which express male supremacy and physical dominance are surely not the paradigms, nor the span nor the height nor depth, of the pleasure available to one living as a male body. There is some intuition of this in gay male culture, and the guardians of male-supremacism do not want it known. A direct and enthusiastic pursuit of the pleasures of the male body will not, I suspect, lead men to masculinity, will not direct men to a life of preying on others and conquering nature, any more than pursuit of bodily pleasure leads women to monogamous heterosexuality and femininity. I can only recommend that men set themselves to discovering and inventing what it *would* lead to.

Another general thing that can safely be said about the resources provided by marginality is that marginality opens the possibility of seeing structures of the dominant culture which are invisible from within it. It is a peculiar blessing both of gay men and of lesbians that in many ways we are both Citizen and Exile, member of the family and stranger. Most of us were raised straight; many have been straight, and many of us can and do pass as straight much of the time. Most of us know that straight world from the inside *and,* if we only will, from its outer edge. We can look at it with the accuracy and depth provided by binocular vision. With the knowledge available to us from our different perches at the margins of things, we can base our inventions of ourselves, inventions of what a woman is and of what a man is, on a really remarkable understanding of humans and human society as they have been constructed and misconstructed before. If only we will. The will is a most necessary element.

It has been the political policy of lesbian feminists to present ourselves publicly as persons who have chosen lesbian patterns of desire and sensuality. Whether as individuals we feel ourselves to have been born lesbians or to be lesbians by decision, we claim as morally and politically conscious agents a positive choice to go with it: to claim our lesbianism, to take full advantage of its advantages. This is central to our feminism: that women can know their own bodies and desires, interpret their own erotic currents, create and choose environments which encourage chosen changes in all these; and that a female eroticism that is independent of males and of masculinity *is* possible and *can* be chosen. We claim these things and fight in the world for all women's liberty to live them without punishment and terror, believing also that if the world permits self-determined female eroticism, it will be a wholly different world. It has generally been the political policy of the male-dominated gay rights movement to *deny* that homosexuality is chosen, or worthy of choice. In the public arena that movement's primary stance has been: "We would be straight if we had a choice, but we don't have a choice" supplemented by "We're really just human, just like you." The implication is that it is only human to want to be straight, and only too human to have flaws and hang-ups. While apologizing for difference by excusing it as something over which one has no control, this combination of themes seeks to drown that same difference in a sentimental wash of common humanity.

For the benefits of marginality to be reaped, marginality must in some sense be chosen. Even if, in one's own individual history, one experiences one's patterns of desire as given and not chosen, one may deny, resist, tolerate or embrace

them. One can choose a way of life which is devoted to
changing them, disguising oneself or escaping the consequences of difference, or a way of life which takes on one's difference as integral to one's stance and location in the world. If
one takes the route of denial and avoidance, one cannot take
difference as a resource. One cannot see what is to be seen
from one's particular vantage point or know what can be
known to a body so located if one is preoccupied with wishing one were not there, denying the peculiarity of one's position, disowning oneself.

The power available to those who choose, who decide in
favor of deviance from heterosexual norms, can be very great.
The choosing, the deciding, challenges doctrines of genetic de-
terminism which obscure the fact that heterosexuality is part
of a politics. The choosing challenges the value placed on
heterosexual normalcy. And the choosing places the choosing
agent in a position to create and explore a different vision.

Many gay men, including many of those in positions of leadership in the gay rights movement, have not *wanted* this kind
of power. They have not wanted any fundamental change of
politics and society or any radical new knowledge, but rather
have only wanted their proper (usually, white male) share of
the booty. But others have begun to understand the potentially healing and revelatory power of difference and are beginning to commit themselves to the project of reinventing
maleness from a positive and chosen position at the outer edge
of the structures of masculinity and male supremacism.

If there is hope for a coordination of the efforts and insights
of lesbian feminists and gay men, it is here at the edges that we
may find it, when we are working from chosen foundations in
our different differences.

NOTES

1. See *Pornography: Men Possessing Women*, by Andrea Dworkin (Perigee Books, Putnam, 1981). And "Sadomasochism: Eroticized Violence, Eroticized Powerlessness," in *Against Sadomasochism: A Radical Feminist Analysis*, edited by Robin Ruth Linden, Darlene R. Pagano, Diana E.H. Russell and Susan Leigh Star (Frog In The Well, 430 Oakdale Road, East Palo Alto, California 94302, 1982), p. 125 ff.

2. See *Woman Hating*, Andrea Dworkin (E.P. Dutton, 1974), and *Gyn/Ecology: The Metaethics of Radical Feminism*, by Mary Daly (Beacon Press, Boston, 1978), especially the First and Second Passages, for full discussion of the symptoms and functions of woman-hating.

3. Thanks to C.S. for the realization that gay effeminacy has so little to do with women that it is not even primarily the mockery of women I had thought it was.

4. This observation due to C.S.

5. This point due to John Stoltenberg. See "Toward Gender Justice," *WIN Magazine*, March 20, 1975, pp. 6-9.

6. See "Sexist Slang and the Gay Community: Are You One, Too?" by Julia P. Stanley and Susan W. Robbins, *The Michigan Occasional Papers Series*, Number XIV (Michigan Occasional Papers in Women's Studies, University of Michigan, 354 Lorch Hall, Ann Arbor, Michigan 48109).

7. For explanation and elaboration of this claim, see "To See And Be Seen: The Politics of Reality," in this collection.

8. That this kind of unconsciousness is one of the privileges of dominance was first made clear to me by Regi Teasley, long before (to my knowledge) other feminists had understood it.

TO BE AND BE SEEN: THE POLITICS OF REALITY*

I

In the Spring of 1978, at a meeting of the Midwestern Division of the Society for Women in Philosophy, Sarah Hoagland read a paper entitled "Lesbian Epistemology," in which she sketched the following picture:

> In the conceptual schemes of phallocracies there is no category of woman-identified-woman, woman-loving-woman or woman-centered-woman; that is, there is no such thing as a lesbian. This puts a lesbian in the interesting and peculiar position of being something that doesn't exist, and this position is a singular vantage point with respect to the reality which does not include her. It affords her a certain freedom from constraints of the conceptual system; it gives her access to knowledge which is inaccessible to those whose

---

* This is a very slightly revised version of the essay which appeared in *Sinister Wisdom 17* with the title, "To Be And Be Seen: Metaphysical Misogyny."

existence *is* countenanced by the system. Lesbians
can therefore undertake kinds of criticism and description, and kinds of intellectual invention, hitherto
unimagined.

Hoagland was urging lesbian-feminists to begin this work, and
she did not try to say in advance what could be seen from
that exceptional epistemic position.

Some critics of that paper, bridling at the suggestion that
lesbians might be blessed with any exotic powers or special
opportunities, were quick to demand a definition of the word
'lesbian'. They knew that if a definition of 'lesbian' featured
certain patterns of physical contacts as definitive, then the
claim that phallocratic conceptual schemes do not include
lesbians would be obviously false, since phallocrats obviously
can and do wrap their rapacious minds around verbal and
visual images of females so positioned physically, with respect
to each other. And they knew also, on the other hand, that
any definition which is more "spiritual," such as *woman-iden-
tified-woman,* will be flexible enough to permit almost any
woman to count herself a lesbian and claim for herself these
exciting epistemological privileges.

Other critics, who found Hoagland's picture engaging but
were loathe to glorify the conditions of exile, pressed for a
definition of 'lesbian' which would be both accurate and illuminating—a definition which would shed light on what it
means to say lesbians are excluded from phallocratic conceptual schemes, and which might even provide some clue as to
what lesbians might see from this strange non-location beyond the pale.

These pressures combined with the philosopher's constitu-
tional propensity to view all orderly procedure as beginning
with definitions, and the assembly was irresistibly drawn into
trying to define the term 'lesbian'. But to no avail. That term
is extraordinarily resistant to standard procedures of semantic
analysis. It finally dawned on me that the elusiveness of the
meaning of the term was itself a clue that Hoagland's picture

was right. If indeed lesbians' existence is not countenanced by the dominant conceptual scheme, it would follow that we could not construct a definition of the term 'lesbian' of the sort we might recommend to well-intentioned editors of dictionaries. If a conceptual scheme excludes something, the standard vocabulary of those whose scheme it is will not be adequate to the defining of a term which denotes it. If Hoagland's picture is right, then whatever we eventually do by way of defining the word 'lesbian', that definition will evolve within a larger enterprise and cannot be the *beginning* of understanding and assessing that picture.

Another way of beginning is suggested by the observation that women of all stripes and colors, including lesbians but also including nonlesbians, suffer erasure. This is true, but it also seems to me that Hoagland is right: the exclusion of lesbians from phallocratic reality is different and is related to unusual knowing. The difficulty lies in trying to say just what this *means*. In order to get a handle on this we need to explore the differences and the connections between the erasure of women generally and the erasure of lesbians.

This inquiry, about what is *not* encompassed by a conceptual scheme, presents problems which arise because the scheme in question is, at least in the large, the inquirer's own scheme. The resources for the inquiry are, in the main, drawn from the very scheme whose limits we are already looking beyond in order to conceive the project. This undertaking therefore engages me in a sort of flirtation with meaninglessness—dancing about a region of cognitive gaps and negative semantic spaces,[1] kept aloft only by the rhythm and momentum of my own motion, trying to plumb abysses which are generally agreed not to exist and to map the tensions which create them. The danger is of falling into incoherence. But conceptual schemes have saving complexities such that their structures and substructures imitate and reflect each other and one thus can locate holes and gaps indirectly which cannot, in the nature of the thing, be directly named.

I start with a semantic reminder.

II

Reality is that which is.

The English word 'real' stems from a word which meant *regal*, of or pertaining to the king.

'Real' in Spanish means *royal*.

Real property is that which is proper to the king.

Real estate is the estate of the king.

Reality is that which pertains to the one in power, is that over which he has power, is his domain, his estate, is proper to him.

The ideal king reigns over everything as far as the eye can see. His eye. What he cannot see is not royal, not real.

He sees what is proper to him.

To be real is to be visible to the king.

The king is in his counting house.

III

I say, "I am a lesbian. The king does not count lesbians. Lesbians are not real. There are no lesbians." To say this, I use the word 'lesbian', and hence one might think that there is a word for this thing, and thus that the thing must have a place in the conceptual scheme. But this is not so. Let me take you on a guided tour of a few standard dictionaries, to display some reasons for saying that lesbians are not named in the lexicon of the King's English.

If you look up the word 'lesbian' in *The Oxford English Dictionary*, you find an entry that says it is an adjective that means *of or pertaining to the island of Lesbos,* and an entry describing at length and favorably an implement called a lesbian rule, which is a flexible measuring device used by carpenters. Period.

Webster's Third International offers a more pertinent definition. It tells us that a lesbian is a homosexual female. And going on, one finds that 'homosexual' means *of or pertaining to the same sex.* The elucidating example provided is the phrase 'homosexual twins' which means *same-sex twins.* The alert scholar can conclude that a lesbian is a same-sex female.

A recent edition of *Webster's Collegiate Dictionary* tells us that a lesbian is a woman who has sex, or sexual relations, with other women. Such a definition would be accepted by many speakers of the language and at least seems to be coherent, even if too narrow. But the appearance is deceptive, for this account collapses into nonsense, too. The key word in this definition is 'sex': having sex or having sexual relations. But what is having sex? It is worthwhile to follow this up because the pertinent dictionary entries obscure an important point about the logic of sex. Getting clear about that point helps one see that there is semantic closure against recognition of the existence of lesbians, and it also prepares the way for understanding the connection between the place of *woman* and the place of *lesbian* with respect to the phallocratic scheme of things.[2]

Dictionaries generally agree that 'sexual' means something on the order of *pertaining to the genital union of a female and a male animal,* and that "having sex" is having intercourse —intercourse being defined as the penetration of a vagina by a penis, with ejaculation. My own observation of usage leads me to think these accounts are inadequate and misleading. Some uses of these terms do fit this dictionary account. For instance, parents and counselors standardly remind young women that if they are going to be sexually active they must deal responsibly with the possibility of becoming pregnant. In this context, the word 'sexually' is pretty clearly being used in a way that accords with the given definition. But many activities and events fall under the rubric 'sexual', apparently without semantic deviance, though they do not involve penile penetration of the vagina of a female human being. Penile penetration of almost anything, especially if it is accompanied by ejaculation, counts as having sex or being sexual. Moreover, events which cannot plausibly be seen as pertaining to penile erection, penetration and ejaculation will, in general, not be counted as sexual, and events that do not involve penile penetration or ejaculation will not be counted as having sex. For instance, if a girlchild is fondled and aroused by a man, and comes to orgasm, but the man refrains from penetration and ejaculation, the man can say, and speakers of English will generally agree, that he did not have sex with her. No matter what is going on, or (it must be mentioned) *not* going on, with respect to female arousal or orgasm, or in connection with the vagina, a pair can be said without semantic deviance to have had sex, or not to have had sex; the use of that term turns entirely on what was going on with respect to the penis.

When one first considers the dictionary definitions of 'sex' and 'sexual', it seems that all sexuality is heterosexuality, by definition, and that the term 'homosexual' would be internally contradictory. There are uses of the term according to which this is exactly so. But in the usual and standard use, there is nothing semantically odd in describing two men as having sex with each other. According to that usage, any situation in which one or more penises are present is one in which something could happen which could be called having sex. But on this apparently "broader" definition there is nothing women could do in the absence of men that could, without semantic oddity, be called "having sex." Speaking of women who have sex with other women is like speaking of ducks who engage in arm wrestling.

When the dictionary defines lesbians as women who have sex or sexual relations with other women, it defines lesbians as logically impossible.

Looking for other words in the lexicon which might denote these beings which are non-named 'lesbians', one thinks of terms in the vernacular, like 'dyke', 'bulldagger' and so on. Perhaps it is just as well that standard dictionaries do not pretend to provide relevant definitions of such terms. Generally, these two terms are used to denote women who are perceived as imitating, dressing up like, or trying to be men. Whatever the extent of the class of women who are perceived to do such things, it obviously is not coextensive with the class of lesbians. Nearly every feminist, and many other women as well, have been perceived as wishing to be men, and a great many lesbians are not so perceived. The term 'dyke' has been appropriated by some lesbians as a term of pride and solidarity, but in that use it is unintelligible to most speakers of English.

One of the current definitions of 'lesbianism' among lesbians is *woman-loving*—the polar opposite of misogyny. Several dictionaries I checked have entries for 'misogyny' (hatred of women), but not for 'philogyny' (love of women). I found one which defines 'philogyny' as *fondness for women,* and another dictionary defines 'philogyny' as *Don Juanism.* Obviously neither of these means *love of women* as it is intended by lesbians combing the vocabulary for ways to refer to themselves. According to the dictionaries, there is no term in English for the polar opposite of misogyny nor for persons whose characteristic orientation toward women is the polar opposite of misogyny.

Flinging the net wider, one can look up the more Victorian words, like sapphism and sapphist. In *Webster's Collegiate,* 'sapphism' is defined just as *lesbianism.* But *The Oxford English Dictionary* introduces another twist. Under the heading of 'sapphism' is an entry for 'sapphist' according to which sapphists are those addicted to unnatural sexual relations between women. The fact that these relations are characterized as unnatural is revealing. For what is unnatural is contrary to the laws of nature, or contrary to the nature of the substance of entity in question. But what is contrary to the laws of nature cannot happen: that is what it means to call these laws the laws of nature. And I cannot do what is contrary to my nature, for if I could do it, it would be in my nature to do it. To call something "unnatural" is to say it cannot be. This definition defines sapphists, that is lesbians, as *naturally* impossible as well as *logically* impossible.

The notion that lesbianism is not possible in nature, that it is nobody's nature to be a lesbian, has a life of its own even among some people who do know factually that there are certain women who do and are inclined to do certain things with other women and who sincerely avow certain feelings and attitudes toward women. Lesbianism can be seen as not natural in that if someone lives as a lesbian, it is not assumed that that is just who, or how, she *is*. Rather, it is presumed to be some sort of affliction, or is a result of failed attempts to solve some sort of problem or resolve some sort of conflict (and if she could find another way, she would take it, and then would not be a lesbian). Being a lesbian is understood as something which could be nobody's natural configuration but must be a configuration one is twisted into by some sort of force which is in some basic sense "external" to one. "Being a lesbian" is understood here as certain sorts of people understand "being a delinquent" or "being an alcoholic." It is not of one's nature the way illness is not of one's nature. To see this sense of "unnatural," one can contrast it with the presumed "naturalness" of the heterosexuality of women. As most people see it, being heterosexual is just being. It is not *interpreted*. It is not understood as a consequence of anything. It is not viewed as possibly a solution to some problem, or as a way of acting and feeling which one worked out or was pushed to by circumstances. On this sort of view, all women *are* heterosexual, and some women somehow come to *act* otherwise. On this view, no one *is*, in the same sense, a lesbian.

There are people who do believe in the real existence of perverts and deviants. What they share with those who do not is the view that the behaviors and attitudes in question are not natural to *humans*. One's choice then, when confronted with someone who says she is a lesbian, is to believe her and class her as not fully or really human, or to class her as fully and really human and not believe that she is a lesbian.

Lesbian.
One of the people of the Isle of Lesbos.

It is bizarre that when I try to name myself and explain myself, my native tongue provides me with a word that is so foreign, so false, so hopelessly inappropriate. Why am I referred to by a term which means *one of the people of Lesbos?*

The use of the word 'lesbian' to name us is a quadrifold evasion, a laminated euphemism. To name us, one goes by way of a reference to the island of Lesbos, which in turn is an indirect reference to the poet Sappho (who used to live there, they say), which in turn is itself an indirect reference to what fragments of her poetry have survived a few millenia of patriarchy, and this in turn (if we have not lost you by now) is a prophylactic avoidance of direct mention of the sort of creature who would write such poems or to whom such poems would be written. . .assuming you happen to know what is in those poems written in a dialect of Greek over two thousand five hundred years ago on some small island somewhere in the wine dark Aegean Sea.

This is a truly remarkable feat of silence.

The philosopher John Langshaw Austin, commenting on the connection between language and conceptions of reality, said the following: "Our common stock of words embodies all the distinctions men have found worth drawing, and the connections they have found worth marking, in the lifetimes of many generations."[3]

    our

    common stock of words

    men have found

    distinction is not worth drawing
    connection is not worth marking

Revealing as this is, it still dissembles. It is not that the connections and distinctions are not worth drawing and marking,
it is that men do not want to draw and mark them, or do not
dare to.

IV

When one says that some thing or some class is not countenanced by a certain conceptual scheme, or that it is not
"among the values over which the variables of the system
range," or that it is not among the ontological commitments
of the system, there are at least three things this can mean.
One is just that there is no simple direct term in the system
for the thing or class, and no very satisfactory way to explain
it. For example, it is in this sense that Western conceptual
schemes do not countenance the forces or arrangements called
"karma." Indeed, I don't know whether it is suitable to say
"forces or arrangements" here, and that is part of the point.
A second thing that can be meant when it is said that something is not in the scope of the concepts of the scheme is
that the term which ostensibly denotes the thing is internally
self-contradictory, as in the case of round squares. Nothing
can be in both the class denoted by 'round' and the class denoted by 'square', given what those words mean. A third
thing one can mean when one says a scheme does not encom-
pass a certain thing is that according to principles which are
fundamental to the most general picture of how things are in

the world, the thing could not exist in nature. An example of this is the denial that there could be a beast which was a cross between a dog and a cat. The belief that such a thing could exist would be inconsistent with beliefs about the nature of the world and of animals which underlie vast chunks of the rest of our world view.

Lesbian is the only class I have ever set out to define, the only concept I have ever set out to explain, that seemed to be shut out in more than one of these ways. As the considerations reviewed here seem to show, it is shut out in all three. You can "not believe in lesbians" as you don't believe in the possibility of "doggie-cats" or as you don't believe in round squares; or you can be just unable to accommodate lesbianism in the way I cannot accommodate the notion of Karma— it doesn't articulate suitably with the rest of my concepts; it can't be worked into my active conceptual repertoire.

The redundancy of the devices of closure which are in place here is one of the things which leads me to say that lesbians are *excluded* from the scheme. The overdetermination, the metaphysical overkill, signals a manipulation, a scurrying to erase, to divert the eye, the attention, the mind. Where there is manipulation there is motivation, and it does not seem plausible to me that the reason lies with the physical details of certain women's private lives. The meaning of this erasure and of the totality and conclusiveness of it has to do, I think, with the maintenance of phallocratic reality as a whole, and with the situation of women generally *a propos* that reality.

V

At the outset I said lesbians are not real, that there are no lesbians. I want to say also that women in general are not countenanced by the phallocratic scheme, are not real; there are no women. But the predicament of women *a propos* the

dominant reality is complex and paradoxical, as is revealed in
women's mundane experience of the seesaw of demand and
neglect, of being romanced and assaulted, of being courted
and being ignored. The observations which lead me to say
there are no women in phallocratic reality themselves also begin to reveal the elements of the paradox. These observations
are familiar to feminists; they are among the things we come
back to again and again as new layers of their meanings become accessible to our understanding.

There are two kinds of erasure of women which have by
now become "often noted." One is the conception of human
history as a history of the acts and organizations of men, and
the other is a long and sordid record in western civilization of
the murder and mutilation of women. Both of these erasures
are extended into the future, the one in fiction and speculation, the other in the technological projects of sperm selection
for increasing the proportion of male babies, of extrauterine
gestation, of cloning, of male to female transsexual reconstruction. Both sorts of erasure seem entwined in the pitched religious and political battle between males who want central-
ized male control of female reproductive functions, and males
who want individualized male control of female reproductive
functions. (I speak of the fights about abortion, forced sterilization, the conditions of birthing, etc.)

A reasonable person might think that these efforts to erase
women reveal an all-too-vivid recognition that there *are* wom-
en—that the projects of ideological and material elimination
of women presuppose belief in the existence of the objects to
be eliminated. In a way, I agree. But also, there is a peculiar
mode of relating belief and action which I think is characteristic of the construction of phallocratic reality, according to
which a project of annihilation can be seen to presuppose the
nonexistence of the objects being eliminated. This mode is an
insane reversal of the reasonable procedure of adjusting one's
views so that they accord with reality as actively discovered:
it is a mode according to which one begins with a firmly held
view, composed from fabulous images of oneself, and adopts

as one's project the alteration of the world to bring it into accord with that view.

A powerful example of this strange practice was brought to my attention by Harriet Desmoines who had been reading about the United States' expansion across the North American continent. It seems that the white men, upon encountering the vast and rich midcontinental prairie, called the prairie a *desert*. They conceived a desert, they took it to be a desert, and a century later it is a desert (a fact which is presently somewhat obscured by the annual use of megatons of chemical fertilizers). Did they *really* believe that what they were seeing was a desert? It is a matter of record that that is what they *said* they saw.

There is another example of this sort of practice to be found in the scientific and medical realm, which was brought to my attention by the work of Eileen Van Tassell. It is a standard assumption in the disciplines of human biology and human medicine that the species consists of two sexes, male and female. Concrete physical evidence that there are individuals of indeterminate sex and that "sex-characteristics" occur in spectrums and not as all-or-nothing phenomena is not acknowledged as existent evidence but is removed, erased, through chemical and surgical "cures" and "corrections."[4] In this case, as in the case of the rich and living prairie, erasure of fact and destruction of concrete objects does not demonstrate recognition of the fact or object; it is, on the contrary, direct manifestation of the belief that those are not the facts and the belief that no such individual objects exist.

If it is true that this mode of connection of belief and action is characteristic of phallocratic culture, then one can construct or reconstruct beliefs which are fundamental to that culture's conceptual/scientific system by inspecting the culture's projects and reasoning that what is believed is what the projects would make to be true. As noted before, there are and have long been ongoing projects whose end will be a world with no women in it. Reasoning back, one can conclude that those whose projects these are believe there are no women.

For many of us, the idea that there are no women, that we do not exist, began to dawn when we first grasped the point about the nongeneric so-called "generic" 'man'. The word 'woman' was supposed to mean *female of the species,* but the name of the species is 'Man'. The term 'female man' has a tension of logical impossibility about it that is absent from parallel terms like 'female cat' and 'female terrier'. It makes one suspect that the concept of the species which is operative here is one according to which there are no females of the species. I think one can begin to get a handle on what this means by seeing how it meshes with another interesting phenomenon, namely the remarkable fact that so many men from so many stations in life have so often declared that women are unintelligible to them.

Reading or hearing the speeches of men on the unintelligibility of women, I imagine the men are like people who for some reason can see everything but automobiles and are constantly and painfully perplexed by blasts and roars, thumps and bumps, which they cannot avoid, control or explain. But it is not quite like that, for such men do seem to recognize our physical existence, or at least the existence of some of our parts. What they do not see is our souls.

The phallocratic scheme does not admit women as authors of perception, as seers. Man understands his own perception as simultaneously generating and being generated by a point of view. Man is understood to author names; men have a certain status as points of intellectual and perceptual origin. Insofar as the phallocratic scheme permits the understanding that women perceive at all, it features women's perceptions as passive, repetitive of men's perception, nonauthoritative. Aristotle said it outright: Women are rational, but do not have authority.[5]

Imagine two people looking at a statue, one from the front, the other from the back, and imagine that the one in front

thinks the one in back must be seeing exactly what he is seeing. He cannot fathom how the other can come up with a description so different from his own. It is as though women
are assumed to be robots hooked up to the senses of men—
not using senses of our own, not authoring perception, not
having and generating a point of view. And then they cannot
fathom how we must be wired inside, that we could produce
the output we produce from the input they assume to be
identical with their own. The hypothesis that we are seeing
from a different point of view, and hence simply seeing something he cannot see, is not available to a man, is not in his
repertoire, so long as his total conception of the situation includes a conception of women as not authoritative perceivers
like himself, that is, so long as he does not count women as
men. And no wonder such a man finds women incomprehensible.

VI

For the reasons given, and in the ways indicated, I think
there is much truth in the claim that the phallocratic scheme
does not include women. But while women are erased in history and in speculation, physically liquidated in gynocidal
purges and banished from the community of those with perceptual and semantic authority, we are on the other hand
regularly and systematically invited, seduced, cajoled, coerced
and even paid to be in intimate and constant association with
men and their projects. In this, the situation of women generally is radically different from the situation of lesbians.
Lesbians are not invited to join—the family, the party, the
project, the procession, the war effort. There is a place for a
woman in every game. Wife, secretary, servant, prostitute,
daughter, assistant, babysitter, mistress, seamstress, proof-

reader, nurse, confidante, masseusse, indexer, typist, mother. Any of these is a place for a woman, and women are much encouraged to fill them. None of these is a place for a lesbian.

The exclusion of women from the phallocratic scheme is impressive, frightening and often fatal, but it is not simple and absolute. Women's existence is both absolutely necessary to and irresolvably problematic for the dominant reality and those committed to it, for our existence is *presupposed* by phallocratic reality, but it is not and cannot be *encompassed* by or countenanced by that reality. Women's existence is a background against which phallocratic reality is a foreground.

A foreground scene is created by the motion of foreground figures against a static background. Foreground figures are perceptible, are defined, have identity, only in virtue of their movement against a background. The space in which the motion of foreground figures takes place is created and defined by their movement with respect to each other and against the background. But nothing of the background is *in* or is *part of* or is *encompassed by* the foreground scene and space. The background is unseen by the eye which is focused on foreground figures, and if anything somehow draws the eye to the background, the foreground dissolves. What would draw the eye to the background would be any sudden or well-defined motion in the background. Hence there must be either no motion at all in the background, or an unchanging buzz of small, regular and repetitive motions. The background must be utterly un*event*ful if the foreground is to continue to hang together, that is, if it is to endure as *a space* within which there are discrete *objects* in relation to each other.

I imagine phallocratic reality to be the space and figures and motion which constitute the foreground, and the constant repetitive uneventful activities of women to constitute and maintain the background against which this foreground plays. It is essential to the maintenance of the foreground reality that nothing within it refer in any way to anything in the background, and yet it depends absolutely upon the existence of the background. It is useful to carry this metaphor on in a more concrete mode—thinking of phallocratic reality as a dramatic production on a stage.

The motions of the actors against the stage settings and backdrop constitute and maintain the existence and identities of the characters in a play. The stage setting, props, lights and so forth are created, provided, maintained and occasionally rearranged (according to the script) by stagehands. The stagehands, their motions and the products of those motions, are neither in nor part of the play, are neither in nor part of the reality of the characters. The reality in the framework of which Hamlet's actions have their meaning would be rent or shattered if anything Hamlet did or thought referred in any way to the stagehands or their activities, or if that background blur of activity were in any other way to be resolved into attention-catching events.

The situation of the actors is desperately paradoxical. The actors are absolutely committed to the maintenance of the characters and the characters' reality: participation as characters in the ongoing creation of Reality is their *raison d'etre*. The reality of the character must be lived with fierce concentration. The actor must be immersed in the play and undistracted by any thought for the scenery, props or stagehands, lest the continuity of the characters and the integrity of their reality be dissolved or broken. But if the character must be lived so intently, who will supervise the stagehands to make sure they don't get rowdy, leave early, fall asleep or walk off the job? (Alas, there is no god nor heavenly host to serve as Director and Stage Managers.) Those with the most intense commitment to the maintenance of the reality of the play are precisely those most interested in the proper deportment of the stagehands, and this interest competes directly with that commitment. There is nothing the actor would like better than that there be no such thing as stagehands, posing as they do a constant threat to the very existence, the very life, of the character and hence to the meaning of the life of the actor; and yet the actor is irrevocably tied to the stagehands by his commitment to the play. Hamlet, of course, has no such problems; there are no stagehands in the play.

To escape his dilemma, the actor may throw caution to the wind and lose himself in the character, whereupon stagehands are unthinkable, hence unproblematic. Or he may construct and embrace the belief that the stagehands share exactly his own perceptions and interests and that they are as committed to the play as he—that they are like robots. On such a hypothesis he can assume them to be absolutely dependable and go on about his business single-mindedly and without existential anxiety. A third strategy, which is in a macabre way more sane, is that of trying to solve the problem technologically by constructing actual robots to serve as stagehands.[6] Given the primacy of his commitment to the play, all solutions must involve one form or another of annihilation of the stagehands. Yet all three require the existence of stagehands; the third, he would hope, requiring it only for a while longer.

The solution to the actor's problem which will appear most benign with respect to the stagehands because it erases the erasure, is that of training, persuading and seducing the stagehands into *loving* the actors and taking actors' interests and commitments unto themselves as their own. One significant advantage to this solution is that the actors can carry on without the guilt or confusion that might come with annihilating, replacing or falsely forgetting the stagehands. As it turns out, of course, even this is a less than perfect solution. Stagehands, in the thrall of their commitment, can become confused and think of themselves as actors—and then they may disturb the play by trying to enter it as characters, by trying to participate in the creation and maintainance of Reality. But there are various well-known ways to handle these intrusions and this seems to be, generally speaking, the most popular solution to the actor's dilemma.

VII

All eyes, all attention, all attachment must be focused on the play, which is Phallocratic Reality. Any notice of the stagehands must be oblique and filtered through interest in the play. Anything which threatens the fixation of attention on the play threatens a cataclysmic dissolution of Reality into Chaos. Even the thought of the possibility of a distraction is a distraction. It is necessary to devise devices and construct systems which will lock out the thought-crime of conceiving the possibility of a direct and attentive focus on anything but Reality.

The ever-present potential for cosmological disaster lies with the background. There is nothing in the nature of the background that disposes it to be appropriately tame: it is not made to serve the foreground, it is just there. It therefore is part of the vocation of phallocratic loyalists to police *attention*. They must make it radically impossible to attend to anything in the background; they must make it impossible to think it possible to fasten one's eye on anything in the background.

We can deduce from this understanding of their motivation *what it is* that phallocratic loyalists are motivated to forbid conceiving. What must not be conceived is *a seer* for whom the background is eventful, dramatic, compelling—whose attention fastens upon stagehands and their projects. The loyalists cannot just identify such seers and kill them, for that would focus the loyalists' own attention on the criminal, hence the crime, hence the object of the crime, and that would interrupt the loyalists' own attention to Reality.

The king is in his counting house. The king is greedy and will count for himself everything he dares to. But his greed itself imposes limits on what he dares to count.

VIII

What the king cannot count is a seer whose perception passes the plane of the foreground Reality and focuses upon the background. A seer whose eye is attracted to the ones working as stagehands—the women. A seer in whose eye the woman has authority, has interests of her own, is not a robot. A seer who has no motive for wanting there to be no women; a seer who is not loyal to Reality. We can take the account of the seer who must be unthinkable if Reality is to be kept afloat as the beginning of an account of what a lesbian is. One might try saying that a lesbian is one who, by virtue of her focus, her attention, her attachment, is disloyal to phallocratic reality. She is not committed to its maintenance and the maintenance of those who maintain it, and worse, her mode of disloyalty threatens its utter dissolution in the mere flick of the eye. This sounds extreme, of course, perhaps even hysterical. But listening carefully to the rhetoric of the fanatic fringe of the phallocratic loyalists, one hears that they do think that feminists, whom they fairly reasonably judge to be lesbians, have the power to bring down civilization, to dissolve the social order as we know it, to cause the demise of the species, by our mere existence.

Even the fanatics do not really believe that a lone maverick lesbian can in a flick of her evil eye atomize civilization, of course. Given the collectivity of conceptual schemes, the way they rest on agreement, a maverick perceiver does not have the power to bring one tumbling down—a point also verified by my own experience as a not-so-powerful maverick. What the loyalists fear, and in this I think they are more-or-less right, is a contagion of the maverick perception to the point where the agreement in perception which keeps Reality afloat begins to disintegrate.

The event of becoming a lesbian is a reorientation of attention in a kind of ontological conversion. It is characterized by a feeling of a world dissolving, and by a feeling of disen-

gagement and re-engagement of one's power as a perceiver.
That such conversion happens signals its possibility to others.

Heterosexuality for women is not simply a matter of sexual
preference, any more than lesbianism is. It is a matter of orientation of attention, as is lesbianism, in a metaphysical context controlled by neither heterosexual nor lesbian women.
Attention is a kind of passion. When one's attention is on
something, one is present in a particular way with respect to
that thing. This presence is, among other things, an element
of erotic presence. The orientation of one's attention is also
what fixes and directs the application of one's physical and
emotional work.

If the lesbian sees the women, the woman may see the lesbian seeing her. With this, there is a flowering of possibilities.
The woman, feeling herself seen, may learn that she *can be*
seen; she may also be able to know that a woman can see,
that is, can author perception. With this, there enters for the
woman the logical possibility of assuming her authority as a
perceiver and of shifting her own attention. With that there
is the dawn of choice, and it opens out over the whole world
of women. The lesbian's seeing undercuts the mechanism by
which the production and constant reproduction of heterosexuality for women was to be rendered *automatic*. The nonexistence of lesbians is a piece in the mechanism which is supposed to cut off the possibility of choice or alternative at the
root, namely at the point of conception.

The maintenance of phallocratic reality requires that the
attention of women be focused on men and men's projects—
the play; and that attention not be focused on women—the
stagehands. Woman-loving, as a spontaneous and habitual orientation of attention is then, both directly and indirectly,
inimical to the maintenance of that reality. And therein lies
the reason for the thoroughness of the ontological closure
against lesbians, the power of those closed out, and perhaps
the key to the liberation of women from oppression in a
male-dominated culture.

IX

My primary goal here has not been to state and prove some rigid thesis, but simply to *say* something clearly enough, intelligibly enough, so that it can be understood and thought about. Lesbians are outside the conceptual scheme, and this is something done, not just the way things are. One can begin to see that lesbians are excluded by the scheme, and that this is *motivated,* when one begins to see what purpose the exclusion might serve in connection with keeping women generally in their metaphysical place. It is also true that lesbians are in a position to see things that cannot be seen from within the system. What lesbians see is what makes them lesbians and their seeing is why they have to be excluded. Lesbians are woman-seers. When one is suspected of seeing women, one is spat summarily out of reality, through the cognitive gap and into the negative semantic space. If you ask what became of such a woman, you may be told she became a lesbian, and if you try to find out what a lesbian is, you will be told there is no such thing.

But there is.

NOTES

1. Phrase due to Julia Penelope Stanley.

2. The analysis that follows is my own rendering of an account developed by Carolyn Shafer. My version of it is informed also by my reading of "Sex and Reference," by Janice Moulton, *Philosophy and Sex,* edited by Robert Baker and Frederick Elliston (Prometheus Books, Buffalo, New York, 1975).

3. From "A Plea for Excuses," *Philosophical Papers* (Oxford University Press, 1961).

4. See Note 3 to "Sexism," in this collection.

5. *Politics* I 13, 1260 a13. My attention was first brought to this by a paper, "Aristotle's Views On Women In The *Politics*," presented at the meetings of the Western Division of the Society For Women In Philosophy, Fall 1974, by Jan Bidwell, Susan Ekstrom, Sue Hildebrand and Rhoda H. Kotzin.

6. This solution is discussed in *The Transsexual Empire: The Making of The She-Male,* by Janice G. Raymond (Beacon Press, Boston, 1979).

ABOUT THE AUTHOR

Marilyn Frye teaches Philosophy, writes, and engages in housework and home maintenance. She has helped run a bookstore, worked in Women's Studies, helped run a lesbian center and is a partner in a small press. Born in Tulsa, Oklahoma in 1941, Frye has lived in the Midwest, on both coasts and in Western Canada. She grew up as the youngest of two daughters in a stable, traditional (but remarkably nonviolent), devoutly christian family.

The author got her Bachelor's degree at Stanford University in 1963, and her Doctorate at Cornell University in 1969, both in Philosophy.

The Politics of Reality: Essays in Feminist Theory by Marilyn Frye is part of The Crossing Press Feminist Series. Other titles in this Series include:

Feminist Calendars

Folly, A Novel by Maureen Brady

Learning Our Way: Essays in Feminist Education, Edited by Charlotte Bunch and Sandra Pollack

Lesbian Images, Literary Commentary by Jane Rule

Mother, Sister, Daughter, Lover, Stories by Jan Clausen

Motherwit: A Feminist Guide to Psychic Development by Diane Mariechild

Movement, A Novel by Valerie Miner

Natural Birth, Poems by Toi Derricotte

The Notebooks of Leni Clare and Other Short Stories by Sandy Boucher

The Queen of Wands, Poetry by Judy Grahn

True to Life Adventure Stories, Volumes I and II, Edited by Judy Grahn